THE PEOPLE OF
D U B L I N
1600 - 1799

David Dobson

CLEARFIELD

Printed for Clearfield Company by
Genealogical Publishing Company
Baltimore, Maryland
2016

ISBN 978-0-8063-5826-0

Made in the United States of America

THE PEOPLE OF DUBLIN, 1600 -1799

INTRODUCTION

By 1600 Dublin had become the most important city in Ireland. It was the administrative capital from which the English kings ruled or attempted to control the island of Ireland. The population of Dublin then has been estimated to be in the region of 7,500 however over the next two centuries, which was a period of relative prosperity and economic development, the population expanded, to about 70,000 by 1700 and reached 180,000 in 1800. During the seventeenth century the population was overwhelmingly Protestant however by the late eighteenth century the Catholics were in the majority which resulted from the movement of population from rural Ireland to Dublin attracted by the economic and social benefits available there. In the seventeenth century there was an influx into Dublin of Protestants from within Ireland, as well as from England, and in late century French Huguenots and Dutch immigrants arrived. These immigrants brought with them industrial and commercial skills which broadened the economic base of Dublin and enabled the introduction or expansion of the textile industries of linen, wool, and silk weaving, also sugar refining and metal work. Dublin in the eighteenth century was the center of government, commerce, finance, and was an important entrepot with trade links with the British Isles, Europe, and across the Atlantic.

This genealogical source book attempts to identify some of the citizens of Dublin between 1600 and 1800 and is based largely on primary sources in Ireland and England.

David Dobson, Dundee, Scotland, 2016

THE PEOPLE OF DUBLIN, 1600-1799

<u>REFERENCES</u>

ABR	=	Ayr Burgess Register
AC	=	Annals of Cork
ActsPCCol	=	Acts of the Privy Council, Colonial
ACV	=	Admiralty Court of Virginia
ARM	=	Madeira Regional Archives, Funchal
BRO	=	Bristol Record Office
C	=	A Census of Ireland circa 1659
CBP	=	Calendar of Border Papers
CHOP	=	Calendar of Home Office Papers
CLRO	=	City of London Record Office
CSPCol	=	Calendar of State Papers, Colonial
CSPDom	=	Calendar of State Papers, Domestic
CSPIre	=	Calendar of State Papers, Ireland
DGM	=	Dublin Guild of Merchants
DCA	=	Dublin Corporation Archives
DLA	=	Dublin Libraries and Archives
DRD	=	Dublin Register of Deeds
EP	=	Emigrants to Pennsylvania, 1641-1819
FDJ	=	Faulkner's Dublin Journal, series
FLJ	=	Finn's Leinster Journal, series
FPA	=	Fulham Papers in the Lambeth Palace Library

GAR	=	Rotterdam Archives
GBR	=	Glasgow Burgess Roll
GM	=	Gentleman's Magazine, series
HMC	=	Historical Manuscripts Commission
HSP	=	Huguenot Society Publications
IC	=	Ireland under the Commonwealth, [Manchester, 1913]
ICJ	=	Journal of the Irish House of Commons
IPR	=	Calendar of Patent & Close Rolls Ireland
IWS	=	Ireland and the War at Sea, 1641-1653, [Woodbridge, 2012]
LRO	=	Liverpool Record Office
LRS	=	London Record Society
MdGaz	=	Maryland Gazette, series
MM	=	The Mariner's Mirror, series
NLI	=	National Library of Ireland
NRAS	=	National Register of Archives, Scotland
NRS	=	National Records of Scotland
PaGaz	=	Pennsylvania Gazette, series
PCC	=	Prerogative Court of Canterbury
PIG	=	Philadelphia Independent Gazetteer, series
PROI	=	Public Record Office of Ireland

PRONI	=	Public Record Office, Northern Ireland
RCPE	=	Royal College of Physicians, Edinburgh
SCGaz	=	South Carolina Gazette, series
SOD	=	State Paper Office, Dublin
SPAWI	=	Calendar of State Papers, America & West Indies
TBB	=	Town Book, Corporation of Belfast
TNA	=	The National Archives
VaGaz	=	Virginia Gazette, series
WCI	=	West Country Intelligence, series
WI	=	Without Indentures, [Rochester, N.Y.]
XJVa	=	Executive Journals of the Council of Colonial Virginia

THE PEOPLE OF DUBLIN, 1600-1799

ABBOTT, ANNE, a widow in Dublin, probate 1692 PCC

ABBOTT, CHRISTOPHER, a smith, formerly an apprentice to Edward Brenford a smith, was admitted as a Freeman of Dublin in 1698. [DLA]

ABBOTT, JOHN, a brewer, was admitted as a Freeman of Dublin in 1696. [DLA]

ABERCROMBY, Captain WILLIAM, died in the Invalid Barracks in Dublin in 1802. [SM.64.276]

ADAMS, Mrs, of Peter Street, Dublin, relict of Counsellor Adams, died in 1766. [FDJ.4122]

ADDERLEY, Miss, of Fleet Street, Dublin, married Samuel Kelly, a Revenue officer, in 1765. [FDJ.3932]

ADEE, FREDERIC, DU MESNIL, from Metz, France, a Huguenot soldier in the service of King William, died 1723, buried in St Patrick's, Dublin. [HSP.XLI]

ADRIEN, PAUL, a merchant, was admitted as a Freeman of Dublin in 1712, [DLA]; a grocer, died in York Street, Dublin, in 1766. [FDJ.4080]

AIKENHEAD, PATRICK, born 1713, a book-keeper from Dublin, an indentured servant bound for Jamaica in 1733. [CLRO]

ALDER, JOHN, a former Captain in Sir John Whiteford's Regiment of Dragoons, died at St Stephen's Green, Dublin, in 1764. [FDJ.3926]

ALDING, PHILLIP, a gentleman in Golden Lane, St Bride's parish, Dublin, 1659. [C]

ALEXANDER, HENRY, a cutler and a member of the Guild of St Luke the Evangelist, Dublin, 1669. [CSPIre]

ALEXANDER, ..., an Attorney-at Law in Capel Street, Dublin. A

1

letter, 1750. [PRONI.D233.15]

ALLEN, Sir JOSHUA, in Dublin, a deed, 1680, [NAI.2000.20.4.4]; co-owner of the Arran of Dublin which was seized by the Governor of Malaga, Spain, in 1684. [CalSPDom.1684.204]

ALLEN, RALPH, in Skinner Row, parish of St Nicholas within the Walls, Dublin, in 1659. [C]

ALLEN, ROBERT, a carpenter and a brother of the Corporation of Carpenters in Dublin, 1656. [DCA.G2/1]

ALLEN, THOMAS, a merchant in Dublin, trading with Cadiz, Spain, in 1601. [CSPIre]

ALLOWAY, BENJAMIN, a merchant, a former apprentice of William Alloway, was admitted as a Freeman of Dublin in 1761. [DLA]

ALLOWAY, JOHN, a shoemaker, former apprentice to John Alloway, a shoemaker in High Street, Dublin was admitted as a Freeman of Dublin in 1809. [DLA]

ALLOWAY, WILLIAM, a Quaker merchant, former apprentice of James Watson, was admitted as a Freeman of Dublin in 1747. [DLA]

ALLOWAY, ..., a merchant in Eustace Street, Dublin, died in 1766. [FDJ.4040]

AMBROSE, JOHN, a miller and a brother of the Corporation of Carpenters in Dublin, 1656. [DCA.G2/1]

ANDERSON, ROBERT, in Little Booter Lane, Dublin, a will, 1772, to be interred in St Andrew's churchyard, Dublin, his wife Mary, his children Thomasina and John, John Carmichael a hosier in Castle Street, Dublin, Jonathan Binns an ironmonger in Castle Street, Dublin, wits. William Jordan, William Mondel, John Hays a painter, and Stephen Malone a woolcomber, all in Dublin. [DRD]

ANDERSON, WILLIAM, a joiner and a brother of the Corporation of Carpenters in Dublin, 1656. [DCA.G2/1]

THE PEOPLE OF DUBLIN, 1600-1799

ANDOUIN, JACQUES DE, born 1662, a Huguenot soldier in the service of King William, died 1723, buried in St Patrick's, Dublin, husband of Ann Perroteau. [HSP.XLI]

ANDREWS, FRANCIS, Provost of Trinity College, Dublin, will and codicil, 1774, refers to Ann Hamilton and her daughter Ann Hamilton, Edmond Sexton Berry, Marcus Paterson, Robert Gamble, William Gamble and his wife Margaret, Mrs Anne Norman daughter of William Gamble, Richard Rigby, and Dolly Monroe, wits. John Monk Mason, William Montgomery, Vaunt Montgomery, John Stephens a gentleman in Dublin, and John Macabe a gentleman in Dublin. [DRD]

ANDREWS, NATHANIEL, a gentleman in Dublin, probate 1678 PCC

ANDREWS, PATRICK, a shoemaker, formerly an apprentice to Symon Russell a shoemaker, was admitted as a Freeman of Dublin in 1674. [DLA]

ANDREWS, SAMUEL, died on Rogerson's Quay, Dublin, in 1764. [FDJ.3822]

ANDREWS, THOMAS, a tallow chandler, formerly apprentice to Samuel Bennett a tallow chandler, was admitted as a Freeman of Dublin in 1682. [DLA]

ANNESLEY, ARTHUR, in Dublin, a deed, 1654. [PRONI.D198.G1]

ARABIN, DE BARCILLE, born in Riez, France, son of Alexandre Arabin and his wife Marguerite, naturalised in 1699, a Huguenot soldier in the service of King William, married Jeanne Renee de Malacare, died 1713, buried in Peter Street, Dublin. [HSP.XLI]

ARBUCKLE, JAMES, in Dublin, will, 1746. [PRONI.T700.1]

ARBUTHNOT, JAMES, an apothecary, married Miss Beauchamp, of Augier Street, Dublin, in 1770. [FLJ.52]

ARCHER, JOHN, a gentleman in St Bride's parish, Dublin, in 1659. [C]

ARCHBOLD, ANDREW, from Dublin, a student at Rheims University in 1685. [RCPE]

ARCHBOLD, JOSEPH, of Vicar's Street, Dublin, married Frances Carberry of Coolough, in 1764. [FDJ.3821]

ARCHBOLD, ROBERT, died in Dorset Street, Dublin, in 1763. [FDJ.3725]

ARCHBOLD, STEPHEN, a barber surgeon, formerly an apprentice to Patrick Archbold a barber surgeon, was admitted as a Freeman of Dublin in 1686. [DLA]

ARCHBOLD, WILLIAM, a goldsmith, formerly apprentice to Stephen Archbold a goldsmith, was admitted as a Freeman of Dublin in 1681. [DRA]

ARCHBOLD, WILLIAM, a baker in Dublin, took the Oath of Allegiance and Supremacy to King Charles II in 1665.

ARCHER, BENJAMIN, a carpenter and a brother of the Corporation of Carpenters in Dublin, 1656. [DCA.G2/1]

ARCHER, ..., a widow and a glazier on Blind Quay, Dublin, died in 1766. [FDJ.4118]

ARMSTRONG, Sir THOMAS, in Dublin, probate 1676 PCC

ARMSTRONG, ARCHIBALD, born 1774, a merchant from Dublin, was naturalised in South Carolina in 1803. [NARA.M1183]

ARNOLD, JOHN, in Dublin, a letter, 1760. [PRONI.D354.350]

ARNOP, Lieutenant Colonel, in Stevens Street, Dublin, 1659. [C]

ARTHUR, Miss, of Abbey Street, Dublin, married Francis Purcell of Crumlin, in 1766. [FDJ.4121]

ASHBURY, JOSEPH, a theatre developer in Dublin, a petition, 1710. [TNA.SP34.31.76].

ASHWORTH, HENRY, a proctor, died in Cabragh Street, Dublin, in 1766. [FDJ.4067]

ASSIN, JOHN, a gentleman, in Stevens Street, Dublin, 1659. [C]

ATHERTON, FRANCIS, a carpenter, was admitted as a Freeman of Dublin in 1685. [DLA]

ATHERTON, FRANCIS, a merchant in Dublin, died in Chester, probate 1690. PCC

ATHERTON, WILLIAM, a smith, was admitted as a Freeman of Dublin in 1660. [DLA]

ATKINS, Mrs, born 1673, a widow, died in Back Lane, Dublin, in 1763. [FDJ.3725]

ATKINSON, JOSEPH, in Dublin, letters, 1790. [NRAS.771.Bundle 536]; a letter 1800. [PRONI.D207.29.19]

ATKINSON, THOMAS, master of the Oliver of Dublin trading with Virginia in 1700. [WI.215/250]

AUCHENLECK, JOHN, a merchant in Dublin, a deed, 1664. [NRAS.3215, Largo pp 8/7]

AUBRESPY, DAVID, a Huguenot soldier in the service of King William, husband of Thoinette Mauron, settled in Dublin by 1714, died 1733, buried in St Patrick's, Dublin. [HSP.XLI.12]

AUBUSSARGUES, JACQUES, Sieur de, a Huguenot soldier in the service of King William, naturalised in 1703, probate Dublin 1720. [HSP.XLI]

AUGER, RICHARD, of Chequer Lane, Dublin, married Miss Paris of Little Booters Lane, Dublin, in 1766. [FDJ.4101]

AVERY, JOHN, in Stevens Street, Dublin, 1659. [C]

AVESSEN, ANDRE DE, DE MONCAL, born in Montesquieu, Haute-Garonne, France, a Huguenot soldier in the service of King William, died in Dublin in 1730, buried in St Patrick's. [HSP.XLI]

AYLEWAY, J. ROBERT, in Dublin, a deed, 1696. [PRONI.D562.818]

AYLMER, RICHARD, born 1658, died in Dublin in 1761. [S.23.558]

BACON, THOMAS, in Dublin, a deposition, 1641. [PRONI.D1923.1.14.AU]

BACON, WILLIAM, a linen draper in Corn Market, Dublin, died in 1763. [FDJ.3725]

BAGGOTT, Captain MARK, a Roman Catholic officer in Dublin, 1693. [Cal.SPDom.1693.16]; licenced to bear arms in 1705. [HMC. Ormonde.ii.475]

BAIGNOULX, PAUL, born in Blois, France, a Huguenot soldier in the service of King William, died in Dublin 1724, buried in St Patrick's. [HSP.XLI]

BAISSADE, ETIENNE LA, DE MASSASA, of Monflanquin, Garonne, France, born 1655, a Huguenot soldier in the service of King William, husband of Rachel Hierome, daughter of the minister of St Patrick's in Dublin, died 1694. [HSP.XLI]

BAKER, JOHN, a bricklayer, was admitted as a Freeman of Dublin in 1651. [DLA]; a bricklayer and a brother of the Corporation of Carpenters in Dublin, 1656. [DCA.G2/1]

BAKER, RALPH, a plasterer, was admitted as a Freeman of Dublin in 1649, [DLA]; a plasterer and a brother of the Corporation of Carpenters in Dublin, 1656. [DCA.G2/1]

BALL, Mrs, died in Bride's Alley, Dublin, in 1764. [FDJ.3930]

BAMBRICK, Mrs, wife of Thomas Bambrick a merchant, died in Thomas Street, Dublin, in 1766. [FDJ.4128]

BANCONS, JEAN, of Le Puch, Gironde, France, a Huguenot soldier in the service of King William, died in Dublin 1726, buried in St Patrick's. [HSP.XLI]

BANCONS, JEREMIE, of Le Puch, Gironde, France, born 1656, a Huguenot soldier in the service of King William, died in Dublin 1722, buried at St Stephens Green.. [HSP.XLI]

BANNER, GEORGE, a butcher in Ormond Market, Dublin, died in 1766. [FDJ.4111]

BANNER, HUGH, a butcher, was admitted as a Freeman of Dublin in 1736. [DLA]

BARBAULT, JACQUES, born 1636 in Dieppe, France, a Huguenot soldier in the service of King William, died in Dublin in 1709, buried in Peter Street, Dublin. [HSP.XLI]

BARCLAY, JOHN, son of John Barclay, a merchant, was admitted as a Freeman of Dublin in 1748. [DLA]

BARCLAY, JOHN, son of Robert Barclay, a Quaker merchant, died in Dublin in 1751. [SM.13.309]

BARCLAY, JOHN, formerly an apprentice to James Crawley, a shoemaker, was admitted as a Freeman of Dublin in 1765. [DLA]

BARKER, FRANCIS, a joiner and a brother of the Corporation of Carpenters in Dublin, 1656. [DCA.G2/1]

BARKER, PETER, an Attorney of the Court of the Exchequer, died in Little Longford Street, Dublin, in 1764. [FDJ.3829]

BARLOWE, JAMES, a gentleman in Fishamble Street, St John's parish, Dublin, in 1659. [C]

BARNARDISTON, NATHANIEL, a merchant in London, later in Dublin, probate 1678 PCC

BARNES, JAMES, in Dolphin's Barn, Dublin, a lease, 1673. [PRONI.D430.198]

BARNES, JAMES, a surgeon, son of Edward Barnes, was admitted as a Freeman of Dublin in 1712. [DLA]

BARNS, JOHN, a cutler, married Miss Johnson, both of Mary Lane, Dublin, in 1766. [FDJ.4108]

BARNES, THOMAS, a merchant, son of Samuel Barnes, was admitted as a Freeman of Dublin in 1737. [DLA]

BARNES, ...a lodger in Sheep Street, St Bride's parish, Dublin, 1659. [C]

BARNWALL, Captain CHRISTOPHER, a Roman Catholic officer in Dublin, 1693. [Cal.SPDom.1693.18]

BARNWELL, EDWARD, born 1784, a mariner from Dublin, was naturalised in South Carolina in 1804. [NARA.M1183]

BARNWELL, MARY, daughter of Sir John Barnwell the Recorder of Dublin, was admitted as a Freeman of Dublin in 1688. [DLA]

BARNEWALL, NICHOLAS, a Roman Catholic in Dublin, licenced to bear arms in 1705. [HMC.Ormonde.ii.475]

BARNWELL, WILLIAM, a merchant, son of Patrick Barnwell, was admitted as a Freeman of Dublin in 1648. [DLA]

BARNWELL, Mr, an apothecary, died in Church Street, Dublin, in 1766. [FDJ.4128]

THE PEOPLE OF DUBLIN, 1600-1799

BARRATT, JOSEPH, a cooper, and a brother of the Corporation of Carpenters in Dublin, 1656. [DCA.G2/1]

BARRET, Mr, a portrait painter in Fade Street, Dublin, died in 1770. [FLJ.52]

BARROW, COLL, in St Bride's parish, Dublin, in 1659. [C]

BARRY, JOHN, a merchant, son of Alderman James Barry, was admitted as a Freeman of Dublin in 1608. [DLA]

BARRY, JOHN, in Red Lion Square, Dublin, a letter, 1804. [PRONI.T2627.2.4.6]

BARRY, RICHARD, an alderman of Dublin in 1611. [CSPIre]

BARRY, RICHARD, a gentleman in Dublin, a lease, 1682. [PRONI.D1618.2.17]

BARRY, WILLIAM, a goldsmith, son of Edward Barry, was admitted as a Freeman of Dublin in 1700. [DLA]

BARTON, BARBARA, a will, Dublin, 1794. [PRONI.T1075.37]

BARTON, CHARLES, in Dublin, a will, 1775. [PRONI.T700.1]

BARTON, JOSEPH, in Dublin, a letter, 1790. [PRONI.D207.28.556]

BARTON, WILLIAM, formerly the Customs Collector of Dublin, 1659. [CSPIre]

BASSET, ARTHUR, in Dublin, was granted lands in County Antrim, 1608. [PRONI.D389.1]

BATEMAN, WILLIAM, a publican on George's Quay, Dublin, will, 1775, refers to his wife Alice, wits. John Priestly, Richard Keane, Peter Dillon, and Edmond McCan, all gentlemen in Dublin. [DRD]

9

BAY, Lieutenant PETER, a Roman Catholic officer in Dublin, 1693. [Cal.SPDom.1693.16]

BAYLY, DOROTHY, a widow in Dublin, will, 1748, sons Lambert Bayly, Charles Bayly, and Edward Bayly, grand-daughter Dorothy Bayly, daughters Dorothea Bayly, Arabella Bayly, and Lucinda Bayly, wits. Richard Sumner a confectioner, William Sumner NP, and his clerk Henry Stearn, James Rooney, all in Dublin. [DRD]

BAYNES, EDWARD, junior, in Dublin, probate 1700 PCC

BAYRE, ROBERT, a merchant in Dublin, was admitted as a burgess and guilds-brother of Glasgow in 1712. [GBR]

BEAGHAM, PETER, in Dublin, a will, 1694. [PRONI.T700.1]

BEAGHAM, PETER, in Dublin, a will, 1782. [PRONI.T700/1]

BEAGHAN, BRIDGET, a widow in Liffey Street, Dublin, a will, 1774, refers to William Lyster in Abbey Street, Dublin, wits. Colley Grattan, Robert Sandys a gentleman, Thomas Bracken clerk to said William Lyster. [DRD]

BEALING, BARNABY, in Dublin, son of Roger Bealing in Drogheda, 1627. [CSPIre]

BEALING, ROBERT, in Sheep Street, St Bride's parish, Dublin, 1659. [C]

BECKETT, JOHN, a bricklayer, was admitted as a Freeman of Dublin in 1654. [DLA]; a bricklayer and a brother of the Corporation of Carpenters in Dublin, 1656. [DCA.G2/1]

BEDELL, WILLIAM, Provost of Trinity College, Dublin, was consecrated Bishop of Kilmore and Ardagh in 1629. [CPRIre]

BEE, JOHN, son and heir of James Bee an Alderman of Dublin, 1629. [CPRIre]

BEECH, THOMAS, master of the <u>Shadwell</u> from Dublin to Rotterdam and Bruges and return to Dublin, via Weymouth in 1689. [CTB.IX.100]

BEJARIE, RENE HENRI, Sieur de Sainte Gemmes, Poitou, France, born 1653, a Huguenot soldier in the service of King William, died 1708 in Dublin, buried in St Patrick's. [HSP.XLI]

BELL, Sir THOMAS, MD, died in Dublin in 1789. [SM.51.621]

BELL, Miss, an aged maiden lady, died in Clarendon Street, Dublin, in 1764. [FDJ.3812]

BELLERS, JONATHAN, a merchant in Dublin, probate 1679 PCC

BELLEW, Captain PATRICK, a Roman Catholic officer in Dublin, 1693. [Cal.SPDom.1693.16]

BELLEW, Colonel, a Roman Catholic officer in Dublin, 1693. [Cal.SPDom.1693.16]

BELORIENT, JEAN, a Huguenot soldier in the service of King William, died and was buries in St Patrick's, Dublin, in 1720. [HSP.XLI]

BENCE, Sir ALEXANDER, in Dublin, probate 1691 PCC

BENNET, JOHN, a Justice, died in Dublin in 1791. [SM.33.49]

BENNETT, RICHARD, a gentleman in Stevens Street, Dublin, 1659. [C]

BENSON, JOHN, a member of the Guild of Brewers in Dublin, 1669. [CSPIre]

BENSON, ...,a gentleman in Golden Lane, St Bride's parish, Dublin, 1659. [C]

BERESFORD, Mrs, born 1691, died in Dublin in 1794. [SM.58.71]

BERGEN, THOMAS, a weaver in Fordham's Alley, Dublin, died in 1766. [FDJ.4074]

BERIAN, ANDREW, from Dublin, a student at Louvain University in 1665. [RCPE]

BERMINGHAM, JOHN, a Roman Catholic prisoner in Dublin, to be released on condition that he moved to Connaught in 1657. [IC.II.918]

BERMINGHAM, PATRICK, a miller and a brother of the Corporation of Carpenters in Dublin, 1656. [DCA.G2/1]

BERNARD, FRANCIS, in Dublin, a letter, 1726. [PRONI.D562.94]

BERNARD, JOHN, in Dublin, probate 1653 PCC

BERRY, ANDREW, a carpenter was admitted as a Freeman of Dublin in 1653. [DLA]; a carpenter and a brother of the Corporation of Carpenters in Dublin, 1656. [DCA.G2/1]

BERRY, JOHN, a gentleman in Dublin, probate 1626 PCC

BERRYES, Lieutenant GILBERT, a Roman Catholic officer in Dublin, 1693. [Cal.SPDom.1693.18]

BERSTOW, JEREMIAH, a merchant in Wine Tavern Street, Dublin, 1659. [C]

BETAGH, ..., in Fishshamble Street, Dublin, died 1764. [FDJ.3835]

BETTIN, JOHN, a merchant in Skinner Row, parish of St Nicholas within the Walls, Dublin, in 1659. [C]

BEWLEY, DANIEL, a Quaker and a chandler was admitted as a Freeman of Dublin in 1715, [DLA]; a merchant in Dublin, a will, 1758, refers to his wife Hannah, his daughter Miriam and her husband William Lapham, his son George Bewley, his son-in-law John Clibbor, his daughter Hannah Bewley, his stepsons Joseph and Ambrose Barcroft, his niece Jane Barcroft, her daughters Jane Byrne and Sarah Smith, his brother-in-law Francis Russell, Garrett Hassen; wits. Richard Thwaites NP in Dublin, William Palmer, Robert Jones, Philip Smyth, and James Smith, clerks to said Richard Thwaites. [DRD]

THE PEOPLE OF DUBLIN, 1600-1799

BIGGAR, GEORGE and MARY, in Dublin, a lease 1720.
[PRONI.D298.6]

BILLINGTON, Dame DEBORAH, a widow in Dublin, a will,
1708.[DRD]

BILLINGTON, WILLIAM, a member of the Guild of Brewers in
Dublin, 1669. [CSPIre]

BILLY, CHRISTOPHER, master of the Spitfire of Dublin trading with
Ayr, Scotland, in 1782. [NRS.E504.4.8]

BINNES, JOHN, a Fellow of Trinity College, Dublin, in 1618. [CSPIre]

BINNS, Mrs, wife of Jonathan Binns an ironmonger, died in Dame
Street, Dublin, in 1764. [FDJ.3801]

BIRMINGHAM, THOMAS, married a daughter of Peter Dailly, in
Dublin in 1749. [SM.12.55]

BISHOP, JOHN, a stocking weaver in Plunket Street, Dublin, married
Elizabeth Purley, of George's Lane, Dublin, in 1764. [FDJ.3811]

BISHOP, ROGER, in Skinner Row, parish of St Nicholas within the
Walls, Dublin, in 1659. [C]

BLACHE BELET, CLAUDE DE LA, a Huguenot soldier in the service
of King William, died in Dublin in 1735, his wife Isabeau Chaussegros
de Mimet, died in Dublin 1706 aged 69. [HSP.XLI]

BLACHFORD, Mrs, relict of Reverend John Blachford late vicar of
Lusk, died in William Street, Dublin, in 1770. [FLJ.49]

BLACK, ROBERT, in Dublin, letters, 1790.1804. [PRONI.D207.28.107;
D207.26.34]

BLACKAND, CHRISTOPHER, a gentleman in Trinity Lane, College
Green, Dublin, in 1659. [C]

BLACKHALL, THOMAS, an Alderman of Dublin, died 1796. [SM.58.361]

BLAINE, Mrs JANE, widow of John Blaine a peruke maker, died in Liffey Street, Dublin, in 1763. [FDJ.3725]

BLAIR, BRYCE, a merchant in Dublin, was admitted as a burgess and guilds-brother of Ayr in 1734. [ABR]

BLAKELY, Mrs, a widow in Myler's Abbey, Dublin, died in 1764. [FDJ.3846c]

BLAKENEY, Major ROBERT, born 1691, brother of Lord Blakeney and father of William Blakeney, died in Stephen's Green, Dublin, in 1764. [FDJ.3817]

BLAQUIERE, Sir JOHN, in Dublin, letters 1798. [PRONI.T2593.9/10]

BLIGH Major JOHN, in Damask Street, St Andrews parish, Dublin, in 1659. [C]

BLIGH, WILLIAM, in Damask Street, St Andrews parish, Dublin, in 1659. [C]

BLITH, JOHN, the former Customs Collector of Dublin, 1659. [CSPIre]

BLOOD, EDMUND, son of William Blood, a merchant, was admitted as a Freeman of Dublin in 1745. [DLA]

BLOOD, THOMAS, son of William Blood, a merchant, was admitted as a Freeman of Dublin in 1741. [DLA]

BLOOD, WILLIAM, a merchant in Dublin, was admitted as a burgess and guilds-brother of Glasgow in 1724. [GBR]

BLOXHAM, MARK, a chandler, formerly an apprentice to Thomas Wilson, was admitted as a Freeman of Dublin in 1753. [DLA]

BLOXHAM, Mrs, wife of Mark Bloxham a chandler in Meath Street, Dublin, died in 1766. [FDJ.4073]

BLUNDELL, RICHARD, a gentleman in Fishamble Street, St John's parish, Dublin, in 1659. [C]

BODDINGTON, Mr, died in Dame Street, Dublin, in 1764. [FDJ.3814]

BODKIN, ROBERT, master of the Harrington of Dublin trading with San Sebastien, Spain, in 1705. [CalSPDom.SP44.390.367]

BOILEAU DE CASTLENAU, CHARLES, born 1673 in Nismes, France, son of Jacques Boileau and his wife Francoise des Vignoles, a Huguenot soldier in the service of King William, settled in Dublin 1722 as a wine merchant, died there in 1723. [HSP.XLI]

BOLTON, JOHN, in Church Street, Dublin, died in 1764. [FDJ.3841]

BOLTON, Reverend THOMAS, in Dublin, a letter, 1722. [PRONI.D562.522]

BOMFORD, JOHN, of Parliament Street, Dublin, and Miss Aghmuty were married in 1766. [FDJ.4131]

BOMFORD, Miss, died in Grafton Street, Dublin, in 1770. [FLJ.52]

BOND, Mrs, wife of Mr Bond a tobacconist in Castle Street, Dublin, -- died in 1764. [FDJ.3839]

BONFIELD, JAMES, of New Row, Thomas Street, Dublin, married Maria Farrell of Thomas Street, Dublin, in 1770. [FLJ.53]

BONTOUS, JACQUES, a Huguenot soldier in the service of King William, died in Dublin 1727, buried in St Patrick's there. [HSP.XLI]

BONVILLETTE, JEAN FRANCOIS DAUTIER DE, bon in Lorraine, France, son of Hector de Bonvillette and his wife Anne de Raquest, a Huguenot soldier in the service of King William, settled in Dublin, married Madeleine de Roaurd, parents of Charles Francois, John Francois, Jean Hector, Marie Anne, Alexander, Jean Maximalian, and Theophile. He died in 1748 and was buries in St Patrick's. [HSP.XLI]

BORDEN, GRYFFEN, in Sheep Street, St Bride's parish, Dublin, 1659. [C]

BORES, SILVESTER, a Roman Catholic officer in Dublin, 1693. [Cal.SPDom.1693.16]

BORRON, NICOLAS, born 1647 in Dublin, enlisted as a horseman of the King's Guard in 1663. [HMC/Ormonde.ii.237]

BOSLEROY, CHARLES DE, born 1644, a Huguenot soldier in the service of King William, died 1724 in Dublin, buried in Peter Street cemetery there. [HSP.XLI]

BOSWELL, HENRY, a staymaker, formerly an apprentice to Samuel Fanton, was admitted as a Freeman of Dublin in 1764. [DLA]

BOSWELL, ..., a butcher in Castle Market, Dublin, died 1764. [FDJ.3837]

BOTTOMLY, WILLIAM, a bricklayer and a brother of the Corporation of Carpenters in Dublin, 1656. [DCA.G2/1]

BOUBERS, DANIEL DE BERNATRE, a Huguenot soldier in the service of King William, settled in Dublin, died there in 1747, buried in St Patrick's. [HSP.XLI]

BOUDLER, JOHN, a gentleman in Trinity Lane, College Green, Dublin, in 1659. [C]

BOULTON, PETER, a gentleman in Dublin, probate 1611 PCC

BOURKE, Mrs, wife of Thomas Bourke a merchant, died in Cow Lane, Dublin, in 1764. [FDJ.3811]

BOURKE, ..., a piemaker in Bridge Street, Dublin, married Polly Power of James's Street, Dublin, in 1764. [FDJ.3929]

BOURNE, RICHARD, a cutler and a member of the Guild of St Luke the Evangelist, Dublin, 1669. [CSPIre]

BOUTIN, JOSHUA, master of the Endeavour of Dublin trading with Charleston, South Carolina, in 1732. [TNA.CO5.509]

BOUYE, JOHN, born in Thouneux, Languedoc, France, son of Jean Bouye, residing in the parish of St Michael in Dublin, naturalised in 1678. [IPR. 30 Car ii.20]

BOY, WILLIAM, master of the Mary of Dublin which was captured by Parliamentary forces when bound from Dublin to Chester, England, in 1644. [TNA.HCA.13.62]

BOYD, CHARLES, in Dublin, a deed, 1740. [PRONI.D288.19]

BOYD, DAVID, a merchant in Dublin, was admitted as a burgess and guilds-brother of Glasgow in 1717. [GBR]

BOYD, Mrs ELEANOR, wife of Andrew Boyd a grocer, died on Temple Bar, Dublin, in 1764. [FDJ.3804]

BOYD, JOHN, a merchant, was admitted as a Freeman of Dublin in 1699. [DLA]

BOYD, JOHN, in Marrion Street, Dublin, a letter, 1806. [PRONI.T2541.1B.3.11.6]

BOYD, PATRICK, a merchant, was admitted as a Freeman of Dublin in 1760. [DLA]

BOYD, THOMAS, a merchant in Dublin, trading with Bordeaux, France, in 1656, imprisoned in 1663. [CSPIre]

BOYLE, NATHANIEL, in Skinner Row, parish of St Nicholas within the Walls, Dublin, in 1659. [C]

BOYLY, JOHN, in Dublin, a lease, 1760. [PRONI.D462.7]

BRADDISH, PHANUEL, a sword cutler on Essex Bridge, Dublin, died in 1766. [FDJ.4107]

BRADDCK, CHARLES, a merchant, son of Charles Braddock, was admitted as a Freeman of Dublin in 1761. [DLA]

BRADDOCK, CHARLES, a linen weaver in Bride Street, Dublin, died in 1766. [FDJ.4074]

BRADY, HUGH, born 1787, a clerk in Dublin, emigrated aboard the Rover of New York, master George Bray, bound for New York in 1805. [BM.Addl.ms35762.103]

BRANN, HENRY, master of the Ormond of Dublin, from Barbados to Holland in 1669. [CSPIre]

BRASSELAY, JEAN, born 1669, from Bize, Haute-Pyrenees, a Huguenot soldier in the service of King William, died 1730 in Dublin. [HSP.XLI]

BRAZILL, THOMAS, a butcher, was admitted as a Freeman of Dublin in 1759. [DLA]

BRAZILL, Mrs, wife of Thomas Brazill a butcher, died on Ormond Quay, Dublin, in 1764. [FDJ.3842]

BREFORT, Mrs, wife of Mr Brefort, died on George's Quay, Dublin, in 1762. [FDJ.3724]

BREMON, CHARLES, Seigneur de Rosset, of Gap, Haute Pyrenees, born 1657, a Huguenot soldier in the service of King William, died 1730 in Dublin, buried at St Stephen's Green. [HSP.XLI]

BREWSTER, NATHANIEL, minister of Christ Church in Dublin, 1656. [IC.II.848]

BRICE, CHRISTOPHER, a merchant, was admitted as a Freeman of Dublin in 1605. [DLA]

BRICE, JAMES, an alderman of Dublin in 1641, captain of a trained band of Dublin in 1664. [CSPIre]

BRICE, JOHN, a merchant, son of Walter Brice, was admitted as a Freeman of Dublin in 1722. [DLA]

BRICE, ROBERT, born 1613, son of Reverend Edward Brice, died 22 November 1676 in Dublin, father of three sons and daughters. [Templecorran MI]

BRICE, RONDAL, born 1643, son of Robert Brice, died 8 September 1697 in Dublin, Member of Parliament for Lisburn. [Templecorran MI]

BRIDGES, Mr, in Stevens Street, Dublin, 1659. [C]

BRISE, Mrs, widow of ...Brise a cabinet-maker in College Green, Dublin, died in 1764. [FDJ.3816]

BROCAS, HARRIOTT, in Dublin, a bond, 1770. [PRONI.D207.19.130]

BRODELIE, JOHN, a scholar at Trinity College, Dublin, in 1618. [CSPIre]

BRODICK, ST JOHN, in Dublin, a letter, 1714. [PRONI.D2707.A1.2.5]

BROOKE, Mrs, relict of Henry Brooke and mother of Sir Arthur Brooke, died in Stafford Street, Dublin, in 1764. [FDJ.3817]

BROOKES, ARMOR, a copper plate printer, died in the Cattle Market, Dublin, in 1764. [FDJ.3804]

BROOKES, WILLIAM, a member of the Guild of Brewers in Dublin, 1669. [CSPIre]

BROOME, WILLIAM, Master of His Majesty's Riding House in Dublin, a memorial, 1781. [PRONI.D207.23.8]

BROUNE, ROBERT, in Sheep Street, St Bride's parish, Dublin, 1659. [C]

BROUNE, THOMAS, in Skinner Row, parish of St Nicholas within the Walls, Dublin, in 1659. [C]

BROWNE, EDMUND, a vintner, husband of the daughter of Alderman Sankey Sulliard, was admitted to the Merchant Guild of Dublin in 1651. [DGM]

BROWN, GILBERT, a grocer of Hawkins Street, Dublin, married Miss Tew of Finglass, in 1770. [FLJ.53]

BROWNE, JAMES, from Zealand, a resident of Dublin by 1622. [IPR]

BROWNE, JAMES, a bricklayer and a brother of the Corporation of Carpenters in Dublin, 1656. [DCA.G2/1]

BROWN, JAMES, a merchant in Dublin, was admitted as a Freeman of Belfast in 1753. [TBB]

BROWNE, JOHN, born in Dublin, a merchant, took the Oath of Allegiance and Supremacy to King Charles II in 1672.; a merchant in St Bride's parish, Dublin, in 1659. [C]

BROWNE, Miss MARGARET, in Fishamble Street, Dublin, died 1764. [FDJ.3846]

BROWN, PATRICK, a merchant in Pill Lane, Dublin, died in 1766. [FDJ.4109]

BROWNE, SAMUEL, in Dublin, a deed, 1674. [PRONI.T1878.14]

BROWNE, THOMAS, a bricklayer and a brother of the Corporation of Carpenters in Dublin, 1656. [DCA.G2/1]

BROWN, WILLIAM, in Dublin, a deed, 1622. [PRONI.D430.129]

BROWN, WILLIAM, a merchant in Dublin, was admitted as a Freeman of Belfast in 1753. [TBB]

BROWNRIGG, JOHN, in Dublin, a letter, 1800. [PRONI.D607A.607]

BROWNRIGG, Mrs, wife of Mr Brownrigg, died on the Blind Quay in Dublin in 1766. [FDJ.4047]

BROWNRIGG, Miss, of Golden Lane, Dublin, married Arthur Hunt of County Wicklow in 1766. [FDJ.4116]

BRUER, RALPH COLEMAN, a gentleman in Golden Lane, St Bride's parish, Dublin, 1659. [C]

BRYAN, JOHN, in Chequer Lane, Dublin, in 1659. [C]

BRYAN, SAMUEL, a clerk in Dublin, died in Chester, probate 1682 PCC

BUCKARTON, THOMAS, in Damask Street, St Andrews parish, Dublin, in 1659. [C]

BUCKNELL, RICHARD, in Dublin, probate 1686 PCC

BUGGINS, ANTHONY, a Cornet in Dublin, probate 1692 PCC

BULL, Mrs, died in Brown Street, Dublin, in 1766. [FDJ.4076]

BULLEN, Reverend THOMAS, in Dublin, a mortgage, 1736. [PRONI.D305.2]

BURCHESS, Mrs, wife of George Burchess an apothecary, died on George's Quay, Dublin, in 1764. [FDJ.3815]

BURGESS, JOHN, in Dublin, a lease, 1777. [PRONI.D366.97]

BURGH, Reverend RICHARD, in Dublin, a mortgage, 1720. [PRONI.D671.D11.1.1]

BURGH, THOMAS, in Dublin, a deed, 1707. [PRONI.D671.3.1.8]

BURGH, THOMAS, in Dublin, a bond, 1782. [PRONI.D207.19.157A]

BURKE, PATRICK, born 1721, a book-keeper from Dublin, an indentured servant bound for Jamaica in 1739. [CLRO]

BURLEIGH, ROBERT, from Dublin, an indentured servant in Philadelphia, 1745. [EP.54]

BURLEIGH, WILLIAM, born 1737, son of William Burleigh in Dublin, a lease, 1751. [PRONI.D556.136]

BURNELL, HENRY, in Dublin, 1611. [Carew ms]

BURROUGHS, Mrs, wife of Edmund Burroughs, died in Peter Street, Dublin, in 1766. [FDJ.4132]

BURROWES, Lady MARY, relict of Sir Walter Burrowes, died in Jervais Street, Dublin, in 1764. [FDJ.3801]

BURROWES, MARY, a housekeeper, died in Hendrick Sreet, Dublin, in 1766. [FDJ.4104]

BURT, Captain, a lodger in Damask Street, St Andrews parish, Dublin, in 1659. [C]

BURTON, Cornett, in Stevens Street, Dublin, 1659. [C]

BURTON, Mrs, wife of John Burton, a house painter, died in Lower Abbey Street, Dublin, in 1763. [FDJ.3725]

BUSH, PAUL, one of the Battle Axe Guards, died in Poolbeg Street, Dublin, in 1765. [FDJ.3932]

BUSTON, STEPHEN, a gentleman in Damask Street, St Andrews parish, Dublin, in 1659. [C]

BUTCHIN, JOHN, a cooper and a brother of the Corporation of Carpenters in Dublin, 1656. [DCA.G2/1]

BUTLER, Lieutenant Colonel JAMES, a Roman Catholic officer in Dublin, 1693. [Cal.SPDom.1693.16]

BUTLER, Captain THEOBOLD, a Roman Catholic officer in Dublin, 1693. [Cal.SPDom.1693.16]; licenced to bear arms in 1705. [HMC.Ormond.ii.475]

BUTLER, Captain WALTER, a Roman Catholic officer in Dublin, 1693. [Cal.SPDom.1693.16]

BUTLER, Captain, a Roman Catholic officer in Dublin, 1693. [Cal.SPDom.1693.16]

BUTLER, WILLIAM, a cutler and a member of the Guild of St Luke the Evangelist in Dublin, 1669. [CSPIre]

BUTTLE, DAVID, in Dublin, a deed, 1765. [PRONI.D552.B.1.1.217]

BYFIELD, CHARLES, from Dublin, died aboard HMS Leopard, probate 1674 PCC

BYRCH, HENRY, from Dublin, a student at Utrecht University in 1669. [RCPE]

BYRNE, CHARLES, from Dublin, died aboard HMS Leopard probate 1674 PCC

BYRNE, CHARLES, master of the Marks and Lady of Dublin trading with Antigua in 1716. [Antiguan Court of Chancery]

BIRNE, DANIEL, in Dublin, a deed, 1671. [PRONI.D509.26]

BYRNE, DANIEL, in Dublin, a Roman Catholic, licenced to bear arms in 1705. [HMC.Ormond.ii.475]

BYRNE, EDWARD, born 1694, died in Strand Street, Dublin, in 1766. [FDJ.4059]

BYRN, JAMES, a worsted manufacturer in Dublin, a letter, 1750. [PRONI.D207.23.28]

BYRN, Lieutenant, JOHN, a Roman Catholic officer in Dublin, 1693. [Cal.SPDom.1693.16]

BYRN, MARTIN, a worsted weaver in Dublin, a letter, 1750. [PRONI.D207.23.29]

BYRNE, PATRICK, a carpenter and a brother of the Corporation of Carpenters in Dublin, 1656. [DCA.G2/1]

BYRNE, Mr, a wool-comber, married Mary Byrne of Kevan Street, Dublin, in 1764. [FDJ.3817]

BYRON, Mrs, wife of Mr Byron a card-maker, died in Meath Street, Dublin, in 1766. [FDJ.4073]

CABROL, FRANCOIS, a Huguenot soldier in the service of King William, probate 1727, Dublin. [HSP.XLI.24]

CAILLAUD, RUBEN, a Huguenot soldier in the service of King William, probate 1732, Dublin. [HSP.XLI.24]

CAILLETIERE, CHARLES DE LA, born 1647, a Huguenot soldier in the service of King William, died 1723 in Dublin. [HSP.XLI.24]

CAILLETIERE, THEODORE DE LA, born 1653, a Huguenot soldier in the service of King William, died in Dublin 1730. [HSP.XLI.24]

CAIRNES, WILLIAM, a merchant in Dublin, was admitted as a burgess and guilds-brother of Ayr in 1686. [ABR]

CALDERWOOD, ROBERT, a goldsmith in Castle Street, Dublin, died in 1766. [FDJ.4071]

CALDWELL, ANDREW, in Dublin, a deed, 1707. [PRONI.D778.34]

CALDWELL, CHARLES, in Dublin, a deed, 1769. [PRONI.D126.1]

CALLAN, PATRICK, a baker in Cook Street, Dublin, married ..... Batchellor, a widow in Cook Street, in 1770. [FLJ.50]

CALVERT, Mrs ELIZABETH, widow of Giles Calvert a bookseller in London, died in Dublin, probate 1675 PCC

CAMPBELL, CHARLES, in Dublin, deeds, 1698/1708; a letter, 1723. [PRONI.D562.42; D778.38; D562.500]

CAMPBELL, HECTOR, a tailor, was admitted as a Freeman of Dublin in 1680. [DLA]

CAMPBELL, JAMES, a merchant, was admitted as a Freeman of Dublin in 1705. [DLA]

CAMPBELL, JOHN, a glover, was admitted as a Freeman of Dublin in 1692. [DLA]

CAMPBELL, LAUCHLAN, born1675, son of John Campbell of Kildalloig, Argyll, educated at Glasgow University, Presbyterian minister at St Mary's Abbey, Capel Street, Dublin, from 1707 until his death in 1708. [F.7.527]

CAMPBELL, PATRICK, a stationer, was admitted as a Freeman of Dublin in 1687. [DLA]

CAMPBELL, WILLIAM, a merchant in High Street, Dublin, son of John Campbell a merchant Freeman, was admitted as a Freeman of Dublin in 1742. [DLA]

CAMPION, WILLIAM, master of the True Amity of Dublin bound for Bilbao, Spain, in 1705. [Cal.SPDomSP44.390.322]

CANDIT, ROBERT, in Damask Street, St Andrews parish, Dublin, in 1659 [C]

CANNING, STRATFORD, in Dublin, a will, 1775, refers to his second son Paul Canning, John Dogherty a gentleman in Dublin, wits. Hugh Dogherty in Dublin, John O'Donnell in Dublin, Richard Wilson in Dublin, Newton McMollen in Dublin. [DRD]

CAPORNE, AUGUSTINE, a carpenter and a brother of the Corporation of Carpenters in Dublin, 1656. [DCA.G2/1]

CARBERRY, Captain JOHN, a Roman Catholic officer in Dublin, 1693. [Cal.SPDom.1693.16]

CARD, Reverend RALPH, died in Dorset Street, Dublin, in 1766. [FDJ.4060]

CARDIFF, ..., a silk dyer in George's Lane, Dublin, married Miss Blunt, in 1766. [FDJ.4112]

CARNAC, PIERRE, born 1665, a Huguenot army surgeon in the service of King William, died 1756 in Dublin, buried in St Patrick's. [HSP.XLI.35]

CARNEY, JAMES, a cooper and a brother of the Corporation of Carpenters in Dublin, 1656. [DCA.G2/1]

CARNEY, RICHARD, a limner, was admitted as a Freeman of Dublin in 1656. [DLA]; a painter/stainer and a member of the Guild of St Luke the Evangelist in Dublin, 1669. [CSPIre]

CARR, JOHN, a silversmith in Crampton Court, Dublin, married the widow Palmer of New Street, Dublin, in 1764. [FDJ.3924]

CARR, or RADFORE, MARTHA, in St Nicholas, Dublin, probate 1694 PCC

CARR, NICHOLAS, a cooper and a brother of the Corporation of Carpenters in Dublin, 1656. [DCA.G2/1]

CARR, WILLIAM, from Dublin, a student at Padua University in 1697. [RCPE]

CARROLL, CHARLES, from Dublin, an indentured servant in Philadelphia in 1745. [EP.54]

CARROLL, Sir JAMES, son of Alderman Thomas Carroll, was admitted as a Freeman of Dublin in 1610, [DLA], probate 1660 PCC

CARROLL, JOHN, a shoemaker, formerly an apprentice to Henry Russell a shoemaker, was admitted as a Freeman of Dublin in 1600. [DLA]

CARTER, CATHERINE, of College Green, Dublin, married Captain Wills of the Royal Scots Regiment, in 1765. [FDJ.3936]

CARTER, Mrs ELIZABETH, widow of Charles Carter a saddler in Dublin, probate PCC

CARTER, MICHAEL, a saddler on Cork Hill, Dublin, died in 1766. [FDJ.4076].

CARTER, OLIVER, a wine merchant, married Miss Eccles of Kevin's Port, Dublin, in 1770. [FLJ.51]

CARTER, WILLIAM, a glover in Dublin, died in 1766. [FDJ.4076]

CARTER, Mrs, born 1660, great grand-daughter of Archbishop Usher, died in Great Britain Street, Dublin, in 1764. [FDJ.3930]

CARTER, ..., a son of Henry Boyle Carter, was born in Mary's Street, Dublin, in 1764. [FDJ.3788]

CASIER, Captain ROBERT, a rope-maker in Ringsend, Dublin, was admitted as a burgess and guilds-brother of Ayr in 1721. [ABR]

CASSE, ETIENNE DU, born at Castel Jaloux, Lot et Garonne, France, a Huguenot soldier in the service of King William, died in Dublin 1747, buried in St Patrick's. [HSP.XLI.25]

CASSEL, NICOLAS, a Huguenot soldier in the service of King William, died 1730 in Dublin, buried in St Patrick's. [HSP.XLI.25]

CASSIDY, Mrs DEBORAH, died in Britain Street, Dublin, in 1764. [FDJ.3787]

CASTLES, Mrs, wife of Mr Castles a book-binder, died in Dame Street, Dublin, in 1764. [FDJ.3829]

CATELIN, NATHANIEL, the Recorder of Dublin, later second Sergeant at Law, 1627. [CSPIre]*

CATELY, SAMUEL, a grocer, died on the Coombe, Dublin, in 1770. [FLJ.51]

THE PEOPLE OF DUBLIN, 1600-1799

CATHERIE, ELIE DE LA, born 1635 in Normandy, a Huguenot soldier in the service of King William, died in Dublin in 1699. [HSP.XLI.26]

CAVANAGH, JOHN, a bricklayer, was admitted as a Freeman of Dublin in 1738. [DLA]

CAVANAGH, Mrs, wife of Edmund Cavanagh a grocer, died in Phrapper Street, Dublin, in 1766. [FDJ.4120]

CHAIGNEAU, ELIZABETH, daughter of Louis Chaigneau, wife of David Renouard a Huguenot soldier, died in Dublin in 1772. [HSP.XLI.60]

CHALKE, ISAACK, a painter and stainer and a member of the Guild of St Luke the Evangelist in Dublin, 1669. [CSPIre]

CHALKE, ISAACK, jr., a painter and stainer, was admitted as a Freeman of Dublin in 1683. [DLA]

CHAMBERLAIN, JOHN, formerly an apprentice to George Roche, was admitted to the Merchant Guild of Dublin in 1601. [DGM]

CHAMBERS, JAMES, a glazier, died in Arran Lane, Dublin, in 1766. [FDJ.4125]

CHANGUION, SAMUEL DE, born 1635, a Huguenot soldier in the service of King William, died in Dublin 1707, buried in St Patrick's. [HSP.XLI.27]

CHATAIGNIER DE CRAMAHE, HECTOR FRANCOIS, a Huguenot soldier in the service of King William, died 1725 in Dublin, buried in St Patrick's. [HSP.XLI.27]

CHESHAM, ROBERT, a cooper and a brother of the Corporation of Carpenters in Dublin, 1656. [DCA.G2/1]

CHIPSEY, EDMUND, a silk dyer in Dublin, probate 1698 PCC

CHIPSEY, SAMUEL, a joiner, son of Edmund Chipsey, was admitted as a Freeman of Dublin in 1715. [DLA]

CHOOKE, ISAAC, a plasterer, was admitted as a Freeman of Dublin in 1654, [DLA]; a plasterer and a brother of the Corporation of Carpenters in Dublin, 1656. [DCA.G2/1]

CHRISTIAN, Mrs MARY, relct of Thomas Christian a merchant, died on Aston's Quay, Dublin, in 1764. [FDJ.3802]

CHRISTOPHER, CORNELIUS, from Zealand, a resident of Dublin by 1622. [IPR]

CHRISTY, Mr, a merchant in Church Street, Dublin, married a Miss Tommins in 1766. [FDJ.4039]

CLARKE, ANN. In Dublin, a will, 1749. [PRONI.T700.1]

CLARK, ALEXANDER, in Dublin, was admitted as a burgess and guilds-brother of Ayr in 1801. [ABR]

CLARKE, Captain JAMES, a Roman Catholic officer in Dublin, 1693. [Cal.SPDom.1693.16]

CLARKE,......., in St Bride's parish, Dublin, in 1659. [C]

CLAYPOOLE, Captain, a gentleman in Swan Alley, Dublin, in 1659. [C]

CLEARE, ROBERT, was pardoned in Dublin in 1608. [HMC.Hastings.iv.32]

CLEMENTS, ANN, born 1683, a spinster from Dublin, an indentured servant bound for America in 1704. [LRO]

CLEMENTS, ROBERT, in Dublin, a lease, 1717. [PRONI.D366.4]

CLEMENTS, THEOPHILUS, in Dublin, a lease, 1727. [PRONI.366.4]

CLIFF, JOHN, in Chequer Lane, Dublin, in 1659. [C]

CLINCH, MICHAEL, a brewer, died in James's Street, Dublin, in 1766. [FDJ.4141]

CLINTON, NICHOLAS, a merchant in Dublin, father of Mary his heir, 1631. [IPR.594]

COATE, THOMAS, a helier and a brother of the Corporation of Carpenters in Dublin, 1656. [DCA.G2/1]

COCK, JOHN, a silk throwster in Dublin, died in 1766. [FDJ.4046]

COLE, MICHAEL, in Dublin, a deed, 1669. [PRONI.D509.20]

COLEMAN, GEORGE, a mariner from Dublin, was naturalised in South Carolina in 1796. [NARA.M1183]

COLEMAN, JAMES, a merchant in Dublin, was admitted as a burgess and guilds-brother of Ayr in 1715. [ABR]

COLEMAN, JOHN, an attorney in Skinner Row, Dublin, died in 1766. [FDJ.4085]

COLLES, BARRY, a gentleman in Dublin, will, 1785, refers to his daughter Susanna Meredith, John While, Henry Betagh, William Costello, Mary Isabella Costello, Peter Crossan; wits. John Brownrigg a clerk in Dublin, Dudley Davis a clerk in Dublin, George Warren an attorney in Dublin, Joseph Cavanagh a clerk in Dublin. [DRD]

COLLEY, GERRALD, born in Dublin, a gentleman, was denizised in 1663. [IPR]; took the Oath of Allegiance and Supremacy to King Chares II in 1667.

COLLIER, ISAACK, in St Bride's parish, Dublin, in 1659. [C]

COLLIER, JOHN, a linen draper of Wormwood Gate, Dublin, and Miss Dodd of Mary's Lane, Dublin, married in 1766. [FDJ.4131]

COLLINS, RICHARD, a gentleman in Dublin, probate 1683 PCC

COMBES, NICHOLAS, a gentleman in Golden Lane, St Bride's parish, Dublin, 1659. [C]

COMERFORD, Captain FAULK, a Roman Catholic officer in Dublin, 1693. [Cal.SPDom.1693.16]

COMMIN, Reverend BARTHOLEMEW, died in James Street, Dublin, in 1766. [FDJ.4121]

CONALLY, JAMES, in Dublin, a letter, 1789. [PRONI.D562.8105]

CONALLY, WILLIAM, a land agent and attorney in Dublin, letters, 1674-1701. [PRONI.T2825.B]

CONDITE, ROBERT, a distiller, was admitted as a Freeman of Dublin in 1650, [DLA]; a distiller and a brother of the Corporation of Carpenters in Dublin, 1656. [DCA.G2/1]

CONDRON, Captain WILLIAM, a Roman Catholic officer in Dublin, 1693. [Cal.SPDom.1693.16]

CONNELL, DANIEL, from Dublin, an indentured servant in Philadelphia, 1745. [EP.55]

CONNELL, JOHN, an attorney in Liffey Street, Dublin, died in 1766. [FDJ.4041]

CONNICK, WILLIAM, master of the Ellen of Dublin trading with Scotland in 1782. [NRS.E504.4.8]

CONNOLLY, EDWARD, of Ormond Quay, Dublin, married Mrs Dunn of Smithfield, in 1770. [FLJ.53]

CONNOLLY, JOHN, a clothier in Nicholas Street, Dublin, died in 1766. [FDJ.4046]

CONNOLLY, WILLIAM, in Dublin, a deed, 1709. [PRONI.D665.19]

CONNOR, DANIEL, a carpenter and a brother of the Corporation of Carpenters in Dublin, 1656. [DCA.G2/1]

CONNOR, JOHN, a plasterer and a brother of the Corporation of Carpenters in Dublin, 1656. [DCA.G2/1]

CONNOR, WILLIAM, 'one of the Six Clerks', died in Ship Street, Dublin, in 1766. [FDJ.4058]

CONRAN, PHILIP, an Alderman of Dublin in 1601. [CSPIre]

CONYNGHAM, WILLIAM, in Dublin, 1780. [PRONI.D1449.12.667]

COOKE, SAMUEL, in Dublin, probate 1644 PCC

COOKE, WILLIAM, in Dublin, letters, 1786. [PRONI.T2627]

COOK, ..., master of the Success of Dublin trading with New York in 1769. [MdGaz.739]

COONEY, PETER, printer of a Dublin newspaper, a petition, 1802. [PRONI.D207.23.48]

COOPER, AUSTIN, in Dublin, a letter, 1800. [PRONI.D562.16446]

COOPER, EXPERIENCE, a widow in Dublin, will, 1773, refers to her children Edward, daughter Lydia wife of Joshua Clibborne the son of Robert Clibborne, daughters Ann and Sarah; wits. Thomas Jaffray a gentleman in Dublin, Robert Jaffrey a merchant in Dublin, Richard Thwaites a public notary in Dublin, and Samuel Boursiquot a public notary in Dublin. [DRD]

COOPER, JANE, a widow who died in Dublin, probate 1697 PCC

COOPWER, THOMAS, in Dublin, will, 1755, refers to his sister Elizabeth Irwin, and his nephews Christopher and Percival Irwin; wits. Arthur Perrin an apothecary, James Currin a grocer, William Crowe, and John Crowe, all in Dublin. [DRD]

COPE, JOHN, died in Henry Street, Dublin, in 1766. [FDJ.4121]

COREY, SALT., in Sheep Street, St Bride's parish, Dublin, 1659. [C]

CORKERAN, Mr, died in James's Street, Dublin, in 1764. [FDJ.3812]

CORMICK, MICHAEL, a goldsmith in Parliamentary Street, Dublin, married Ann Bean of Cow Lane, Dublin, in 1766. [FDJ.4083]

CORNYN, MARY, a widow in Dublin, will, 1775, refers to Robert Donnelly a gentleman in Dublin, her cousins James Rainsford and his sister Henrietta Gruebear, George Rainsford, William Crowe a gentleman in Dublin; wits. Reverend John Lyon curate of St Bridget, Dublin, Reverend John Rowelen vicar of Santry, County Dublin, Adam Taitt a gentleman in Exchequer Street, Dublin, Robert Jones a gentleman in Dublin, and John Johnston clerk to the said William Crowe. [DRD]

CORRY, Mrs, wife of Captain Leslie Corry, died on St Stephen's Green, Dublin, 1764. [FDJ.3808]

CORRY, ..., son of John Corry, was born in Dawson Street, Dublin, in 1766. [FDJ.4049]

COSGRAVE, NICHOLAS, a helier and a brother of the Corporation of Carpenters in Dublin, 1656. [DCA.G2/1]

COSSLET, CHARLES GRIMKE, in Dublin, a lease, 1800. [PRONI.D566.159]

COTEN, SAMUEL, a cutler and a member of the Guild of St Luke the Evangelist in Dublin, 1669. [CSPIre]

COTTINGHAM, GEORGE, a mercer in Dame Street, Dublin, married Miss Cuthbert of Drumcondra, in 1766. [FDJ.4136]

COTTON, Lieutenant, in Stevens Street, Dublin, 1659. [C]

COUENY, JAMES, a joiner and a brother of the Corporation of Carpenters in Dublin, 1656. [DCA.G2/1]

COULON, JEAN JACQUES, born 1660 in Montaubon, France, a Huguenot soldier in the service of King William, died 1730 in Dublin, buried in Peter Street. [HSP.XLI.29]

COWAN, WILLIAM, and CICELY ROACH, both of Church Street, Dublin, were married in 1766. [FDJ.4109]

COWLEY, THOMAS, born 1621, a seaman from Dublin, a witness before the High Court of the Admiralty of England in 1646. [TNA.HCA13.60.538/374]

COX, WILLIAM, a cooper and a brother of the Corporation of Carpenters in Dublin, 1656. [DCA.G2/1]

COX, ..., a gentleman in Trinity Lane, College Green, Dublin, in 1659. [C]

COYLE, PATRICK, a cooper, was admitted as a Freeman of Dublin in 1656, [DLA]; a cooper and a brother of the Corporation of Carpenters in Dublin, 1656. [DCA.G2/1]

COYMAN, JACK, a merchant in Dublin in 1648. [GAR.ONA.482]

CRAIG, THOMAS, born 1782, an accountant from Dublin, was naturalised in South Carolina in 1815. [NARA.M1183]

CRAINE, Mrs MARY, wife of Nicholas Craine a carpenter in James's Street, Dublin, in 1764. [FDJ.3930]

CRAVEN, Mrs, a widow in Nassau Street, Dublin, died 1764. [FDJ.3836]

CRAWFORD, HENRY, master of the Mary of Dublin trading with the Canary Islands in 1716. [WCI.20.3.1716]

CRAWFORD, JOHN, a merchant in Dublin, was admitted as a burgess and guilds-brother of Ayr in 1770. [ABR]

CRAWFORD, WILLIAM, of Crane Lane, Dublin, married Miss Weld of Dunleary, in 1766. [FDJ.4121]

CRAWFORD, WILLIAM, a merchant in Dublin, was admitted as a burgess and guilds-brother of Ayr in 1770. [ABR]

CRAWFORD, ..., an officer of the Revenue, died on the Customs House Quay in Dublin, in 1765. [FDJ.3933]

CREAGH, THOMAS, master of the Mary of Dublin a doggar, from Limerick to Bilbao in Spain, and return in 1705. [TNA.SP44.393.16]

CREAMER, THOMAS, a carpenter and a brother of the Corporation of Carpenters in Dublin, 1656. [DCA.G2/1]

CREIGHTON, ..., daughter of John Creighton in Dominick Street, Dublin, was born in 1766. [FDJ.4077]

CRESSERONS, CHARLES DE, born 1655 in Caen, France, a Huguenot soldier in the service of King William, died 1738 in Dublin. [HSP.XLI.30]

CREWE, JOSEPH, a baker in Dublin, 1602. [SPI.1602.400]

CROFT, PHILIP, in Dublin, a deed, 1692. [PRONI.D552.B1.1.84]

CROFTON, JAMES, in the Treasury Chambers, Dublin Castle, a letter, 1801. [PRONI.D562.9372]

CROFTON, Lady, born 1684, died in Ann Street, Stephen's Green, Dublin, in 1764. [FDJ.3828]

CROGHAN, Lieutenant JOHN, a Roman Catholic officer in Dublin, 1693. [Cal.SPDom.1693.16]

CROKER, J., in Dublin, a letter, 1749. [PRONI.T2541.1A.1.2.7]

CROMBEY, GEORGE, from Dublin, a student at Harderwyck University in 1708. [RCPE]

35

CROMWELL, EDWARD, was pardoned in Dublin in 1608. [HMC.Hastings.iv.32]

CROOK, ANDREW, printer to the king, on Ormonde Quay, Dublin, in 1695. [NLI]

CROOKE, KATHERINE, in Dublin, a will, 1757, refers to her mother Elizabeth Parry, Mark Nowlan a gentlemen in Dublin, Thomas Throp in Dublin, Reverend Charles Jones, Elizabeth Palmer, Mr Jams a bookseller and stationer in Dame Street, Dublin; wits. Joshua Shepherd a bookbinder in Dublin, Benjamin Doyle a clerk in Dublin, James Lyons a bookseller in Dublin, and Henry White a gentleman in Dublin. [DRD]

CROSBY, Lady in Fishamble Street, St John's parish, Dublin, in 1659. [C]

CROSE, ISAAC, born 1671 in Mazamet, Tarn, France, a Huguenot soldier in the service of King William, died 1751 in Dublin, buried in St Patrick's. [HSP.XLI.30]

CROWE, JAMES, a gentleman in Dublin, will, 1775, refers to his wife Mary, his sons Robert and George, daughter Elizabeth, nephew James Crowe, Francis Upton and Henry Upton gentlemen in Dublin, George Boleyn Whitney; wits. Joseph Ridge clerk of St Peter's parish in Dublin, Thomas Connor a clerk in Dublin, Francis Sullivan attorney in the Court of the Exchequer in Dublin, and Andrew Hehir a gentleman in Dublin. [DRD]

CROWE, STEPHEN, son of William Crowe late of Dublin, and ward of Thomas Bennett in 1627. [CSPIre]

CROWE, WILLIAM, in Dublin, 1632. [IPR.598]

CRUMPHOUT, HUBERT, born 1616, a merchant in Dublin, 1645. [TNA.HCA13.60.204]

CRYCH, JOHN, a gentleman in St George's Lane, parish of St Andrew, Dublin, in 1659. [C]

CUFF, JAMES, in Sheep Street, St Bride's parish, Dublin, 1659. [C]

CULLEN, EDWARD, married .... RYAN, daughter of the late Edward Ryan in Dublin, in 1766. [FDJ.4112]

CULLEN, RICHARD, of New Row, Dublin, married Miss Kelly of the said place in 1766. [FDJ.4099]

CULME, BENJAMIN, Dean of St Patrick's in Dublin, died in Wiltshire, probate 1658 PCC

CUMIN, PATRICK, born 1649, son of John Cumin of Regulas, Moray, graduated MA from Edinburgh University in 1670, minister of a Presbyterian congregation in Dublin before 1690, he died in 1731. [F.1.341; 7.528]

CUNNINGHAM, DANIEL, in Dublin, letters 1705-1711. [NRAS.3955.16.1.21]; a merchant, was admitted as a Freeman of Dublin in 1707. [DLA]

CUNNINGHAM, JAMES, a shoemaker, was admitted as a Freeman of Dublin in 1668. [DLA]

CUNNINGHAM, RICHARD, a merchant, formerly apprentice to George Forbes, was admitted as a Freeman of Dublin in 1700. [DLA]

CURRAN, DAVID, born 1670, from Dublin, an indentured servant bound for the Chesapeake in 1700. [LRO]

CURREN, ..., a grocer in Stafford Street, Dublin, died in 1766. [FDJ.4045]

CURROGHAN, ..., a baker in George's Lane, Dublin, died 1764. [FDJ.3836]

CURRY, CATHERINE, of the Upper Blind Quay, Dublin, married Charles Taylor, in 1770. [FLJ.53]

CURTIS, CHARLES, a bridle cutter of New Row, Thomas Street, Dublin, married Susanna Curtis of said place, in 1770. [FLJ.53]

CURTIS, JOSEPH, junior, a merchant tailor of London, died in Dublin, probate 1694 PCC

CURTIS, PETER, a wine merchant, died in James Street, Dublin, in 1764. [FDJ.3825]

CURTIS, ROBERT, in Dublin, a letter, 1692. [PRONI.D638.22]

CUSACK, JOHN, a merchant in Dublin, 1602. [SPI.1602.400]

DALLWAY, ALEXANDER, in Dublin, a letter, 1694. [PRONI.D162.8]

DALWAY, ELINOR, daughter of Robert Dalway in Dublin, and Andrew Stuart of Easy, County Tyrone, a marriage settlement, 1695. [PRONI.D1618.2.7]

DALLWAY, ROBERT, in Dublin, a deed, 1694. [PRONI.D509.33]

DALMAN, JACOB, born in the Basses-Pyrenees, a Huguenot soldier in the service of King William, died in Dublin 1702, buried in St Patrick's. [HSP.XLI.31]

DALY, DENNIS, a Roman Catholic in Dublin, licenced to bear arms in 1705. [HMC.Ormonde.ii.475]

DAMBOIN, FRANCOIS, born around 1651, a Huguenot soldier in the service of King William, died in Dublin in 1730, buried at Merrion Row. [HSP.XLI.31]

DAMER. JOSEPH, in Dublin, a lease, 1720. [PRONI.D1062.2.1.6]

DANCER, SAMUEL, was admitted to the Merchant Guild of Dublin in 1677. [MGD]; a merchant was admitted as a Freeman of Dublin in 1677. [DLA]

DANIEL, MARY, in Dublin, widow of William Daniel an orace weaver in Dublin, will, 1755, refers to her daughter Elizabeth Shaw wife of

Samuel Shaw an orace weaver, her grand-daughter Isabella Shaw, her son John Daniel, and her daughter Elinor Shaw; wits. Isaac Bently a carpenter, Henry Stearne, and Philip Brew a watchmaker, all in Dublin, [DRD]

DANIEL, Mrs, widow of Rev. Daniel and daughter of Sir George Ribton, died in Grafton Street, Dublin, in 1764. [FDJ.3841]

D'ARCY, Captain, a Roman Catholic officer in Dublin, 1693. [Cal.SPDom.1693.16]

DARCY, HYACINTH, late of Colonel Horn's Regiment, married Mary, daughter of Edward O'Brian, in Dublin in 1766. [FDJ.4077]

DARENES, FRANCOIS, of Montpellier, France, a Huguenot soldier in the service of King William, died in Dublin 1735, buried in St Patrick's. [HSP.XLI.31]

DARLEY, HUGH, a mason, was admitted as a Freeman of Dublin in 1738, [DLA]; a mason and master builder in Dublin, a letter, 1739. [PRONI.D162.31-32]

DARNER, JOSEPH, in Dublin, a deed, 1719. [PRONI.D1062.2.1.6]

DASON, WILLIAM, an innkeeper in St Bride's parish, Dublin, in 1659. [C]

DAULHAT, Mrs, a widow in Fade Street, Dublin, died in 1766. [FDJ.4047]

DAUSON, Mr, and his son John Dauson, in St Bride's parish, Dublin, in 1659. [C]

DAUSSY, DE ST., JEAN, born 1653, a Huguenot soldier in the service of King William, died in Dublin 1703, buried in St Patrick's. [HSP.XLI.32]

DAVIE, WALTER, a merchant in Dublin, was admitted as a burgess and guilds-brother of Glasgow in 1724. [GBR]

THE PEOPLE OF DUBLIN, 1600-1799

DAVIES, HERCULES, in Dublin, a deed, 1694. [PRONI.D509.33]

DAVYE, PAUL, in Dublin, a contract, 1698. [PRONI.D778.26A]

DAVYS, Sir JOHN, in Dublin, probate 1697, Dublin. [PRONI.D569.1]

DAVYS, ROGER, Constable of Dublin Castle in 1632. [CSPIre]

DAWSON, JOHN, married Miss Pimm, at the Dublin Quaker Meeting in Sycamore Alley, Dublin, in 1766. [FDJ.4129]

DAY, JAMES, born 1688, from Dublin, an indentured servant bound for Newfoundland in 1700. [LRO]

DEACLAUX, NOEL, a Huguenot soldier in the service of King William, died in Dublin in 1726. [HSP.XLI.33]

DEANE, JOSEPH, in Dublin, a deed, 1670. [PRONI.T2374.2]

DEANE, Mrs, wife of Joseph Deane of Terenure, died in Sackville Street, Dublin, in 1766. [FDJ.4056]

DE BARRY, JACQUES, born in Mauvezin, France, a Huguenot soldier in the service of King William, died in Dublin in 1738, buried in St Patrick's. [HSP.XLI]

DE BART, JOSIAS, in St Bride's parish, Dublin, in 1659. [C]

DE BART, ..., a gentleman in St Bride's parish, Dublin, in 1659. [C]

DE BLOSSET, PAUL, born in Longefonds, Isere, France, son of Solomon de Blosset, a Huguenot soldier in the service of King William, died in Dublin in 1719, husband of Jeanne Suzanne de Crozat de Creissal.. [HSP.XLI]

DE BLOSSET, SALOMON, Seigneur de Loche, France, a Huguenot soldier in the service of King William, died in Dublin 1719, buried at St Stephen's Green. [HSP.XLI]

40

THE PEOPLE OF DUBLIN, 1600-1799

DE BLOSSET, SALOMON, the younger, born in Clelles, Isere, France, a Huguenot soldier in the service of King William, naturalised in 1709, married Jeanne Marie Chataigner de Cramahe in Dublin in 1722, she died in 1783, he died around 1749, probate Dublin. [HSP.XLI]

DE GAUTERON, GEDEON, born 1652 in Montpelier, France, a Huguenot soldier in the service of King William, died 1711 in Dublin. [HSP.XLI.40]

DE GIGNOUX, PIERRE, born 1646 in Nismes, France, a Huguenot soldier in the service of King William, died 1699, buried in St Patrick's, Dublin. [HSP.XLI.41]

DE HOURS, HENRI, born in Herault, France, a Huguenot soldier in the service of King William, died in Dublin 1733 and buried in St Patrick's. [HSP.XLI.45]

DE LA ANGOTIERE, ABRAHAM, from Poitou, France, a Huguenot soldier in the service of King William, died in Dublin in 1753. [HSP.XLI.50]

DE LA BALME, GASPARD, a Huguenot soldier in the service of King William, died in Dublin 1726, buried in St Patrick's. [HSP.XLI]

DE LA BILLIERE, PIERRE, born 1669, son of Charles de la Cour, Seigneur de la Billicrc of Alt, Gard, France, and his wife Francoise de Quatrefuges, a Huguenot soldier in the service of King William, died 1746 in Dublin. [HSP.XLI]

DE LA BOUCHETIERE, CHARLES JANURE, Seigneur de la Bouchetiere, a Huguenot soldier in the service of King William, died in Dublin in 1720. [HSP.XLI.]

DE LA BOUCHETIERE, CHARLES JANURE, son of Charles [above], a Huguenot soldier in the service of King William, died in Dublin in 1744. [HSP.XLI]

41

THE PEOPLE OF DUBLIN, 1600-1799

DE LA FONTAN, DANIEL, a Huguenot soldier in the service of King William, in Dublin, died 1719. [HSP.XLI.38]

DE LA GARDE, ISAAC, born 1665 in Dordogne, France, a Huguenot soldier in the service of King William, died 1703 in Dublin. [HSP.XLI.40]

DE LA GARDE, PIERRE, born 1638, a Huguenot soldier in the service of King William, died in Dublin 1710, buried in St Patrick's. [HSP.XLI.40]

DE LA LANDE, HENRI, a Huguenot soldier in the service of King William, died in Dublin 1728 and buried in St Patrick's. [HSP.XLI.46]

DE LA LANDE, HENRI DAUNIS, born in Saintonge, France, a Huguenot soldier in the service of King William, died in Dublin 1737 and buried in St Patrick's. [HSP.XLI.47]

DE LA MAR, ANTHONY, died on Wood Quay, Dublin, in 1766. [FDJ.4075]

DE LA MARE, JOHN, in Dublin, licenced to bear arms in 1705. [HMC.Ormonde.ii.475]

DE LA MERE, Major WALTER, a Roman Catholic officer in Dublin, 1693. [Cal.SPDom.1693.16]; licenced to bear arms in 1705. [HMS.Ormonde.ii.475]

DE LA MILLIERE, CYRUS GUINEBAULD, born in Nantes, France, a Huguenot soldier in the service of King William, died in Dublin and buried in St Patrick's in 1729. [HSP.XLI.53]

DE LA MILLIERE, FLORENT GUINEBAULD, a Huguenot soldier in the service of King William, died in Dublin and buried in St Patrick's in 1728. [HPS.XLI.53]

DE LA PRIMAUDAYE, MAURICE, a Huguenot soldier in the service of King William, died in Dublin 1705. [HSP.XLI.58]

DE LA RIMBLIERE, JACQUES FROTTE, from Damigni, Orne, France, a Huguenot soldier in the service of King William, died in Dublin 1727. [HSP.XLI.61]

DE LA ROUSSELIERE, PIERRE POISPAILLE, a Huguenot soldier in the service of King William, died in Dublin in 1731. [HSP.XLI.62]

DE LA SPOIS, AUGUSTE LE GOUX, born 1666 in Blois, France, a Huguenot soldier in the service of King William, died in Dublin 1709 and buried in St Patrick's. [HSP.XLI.47]

DE LA TOUCHE, DAVID DIGUES, born 1671 in Mer, Touraine, France, a Huguenot soldier in the service of King William, died in Dublin in 1745 and buries in St Patrick's. [HSP.XLI.69]

DE LAP, WILLIAM, a merchant in Abbey Street, Dublin, died 1766. [FDJ.4081]

DE MAZERES, ABRAHAM, born 1667 in Oleron, France, a Huguenot soldier in the service of King William, died in Dublin 1714 and buried in St Patrick's. [HSP.XLI.51]

DE MESTRE, JEAN, a Huguenot soldier in the service of King William, died in Dublin 1720. [HSP.XLI.52]

DEMPSEY, Ensign CHARLES, a Roman Catholic officer in Dublin, 1693. [Cal.SPDom.1693.16]

DEMPSEY, THOMAS, in Dublin, a bond, 1698. [PRONI.D476.255]

DE PUYCHENIN, JAPHET GERAUD, a Huguenot soldier in the service of King William, died in Dublin 1729. [HSP.XLI.59]

DERMOTT, ANTHONY, son of Anthony Dermott a merchant on Usher's Quay, Dublin, married Miss Tobin of Dorset Street, Dublin, in 1764. [FDJ.3926]

DERMOTT, JAMES, master of the Mary of Dublin, was captured by a Salee man o' war in 1687. [CalSPDom.1687.387]

DERMOTT, JAMES, a butcher, was admitted as a Freeman of Dublin in 1717. [DLA]

DERMOTT, JOHN, a gentleman, son of Peter Dermott, was admitted as a Freeman of Dublin in 1637. [DLA]

DERMOTT, PETER, an apothecary in Dublin, 1602. [SPI.1602.400]

DE PECHELS, JACOB, born 1679 in Montaubon, France, a Huguenot soldier in the service of King William, died 1750 in Dublin. [HSP.XLI.56]

DE ST AUBAN, JACQUES, born around 1650, a Huguenot soldier in the service of King William, died in Dublin in 1699 and buried in St Patrick's. [HSP.XLI.63]

DE SURVILLE, JEAN, born in Le Vigan, Gard, France, around 1659, a Huguenot soldier in the service of King William, died 1722 in Dublin. [HSP.XLI.67]

DE VALEDA, JOSEPH, born 1636 in Montaubon, Tarn and Garonne, France, a Huguenot soldier in the service of King William, died 1715 in Dublin. [HSP.XLI.69]

DEVAN, Mr, a grocer, died in College Green, Dublin, in 1764. [FDJ.3807]

DE VAN DIERE, CHARLES DROUART, a Huguenot soldier in the s service of King William, died in Dublin in 1723. [HSP.XLI.70]

DE VEROY, ..., a merchant from London, settled in Dublin, trading with the Canary Islands in the 1660s. [CSPIre]

DES VIGNOLES, CHARLES, born 1645, a Huguenot soldier in the service of King William, die in Dublin in 1726 and buried in St Patrick's. [HSP.XLI.71]

DEVINE, THOMAS, a gunsmith in Dublin, and Sally Wainwright of the Blind Quay, Dublin, were married in 1766. [FDJ.4109]

DICKIE, ADAM, master of the Susannah of Dublin, trading with France, 1705. [TNA.SP34.68-69]

DICKSON, HENRY, an officer of the Royal Navy, married Betty Jefferson, daughter of Robert Jefferson a grocer on George's Quay, Dublin, in 1764. [FDJ.3820]

DICKSON, MATTHEW, born 1785, a clerk in Dublin, emigrated aboard the Rover of New York, master George Bray, bound for New York in 1805. [BM.Addl.ms35762,103]

DICKSON, ROBERT, in Dublin, a deed re property on School Lane, Dublin, 1675. [PRONI.D514.2]

DIGBY, JEREMIAH, a merchant on Batchelor's Walk, Dublin, died in 1763. [FDJ.3725]

DIGBY, ..., son of Dean Digby, was born in Henry Street, Dublin, in 1770. [FLJ.51]

DIGNAN, BRYAN, from Dublin, an indentured servant in Philadelphia, 1745. [EP.54]

DILLON, FRANCIS, a weaver, son of Francis Dillon a weaver in Randford Street, Dublin, was admitted as a Freeman of Dublin in 1762. [DLA]

DILLON, GARRET, born 1681, an indentured servant aboard the Providence of Dublin landed in Middlesex County, Virginia, in 1699. [WI.193]

DILLON, HENRY, in Dublin, a deposition, 1641. [PRONI.D1923.1.16C]

DILLON, JAMES, son of Lord Theobald Dillon, was admitted as a Freeman of Dublin in 1762. [DLA]

DILLON, JOHN, formerly a wool merchant in Usher Street, Dublin, died on the Comb in 1766. [FDJ.4097]

DILLON, RICHARD, a gentleman, and his servant Richard Dillon, Roman Catholic prisoners in Dublin, to be released on condition that they moved to Connaught, 1657. [IC.II.918]

DILLON, ROBERT, a woollen draper on High Street, Dublin, died in 1766. [FDJ.4074]

DILLON, Mrs, wife of James Dillon a surgeon, died in Jervais Street, Dublin, in 1764. [FDJ.3814]

DINNING, JAMES, a tailor in Dublin, a lease in 1773. [PRONI.D2433.A1.81]

DIXSON, GEORGE, in Chequer Lane, Dublin, in 1659. [C]

DOBBIN, FRANCIS, in Dublin, a letter, 1800. [PRONI.D572.668]

DOBBINS, VALENTINE, formerly the Customs Collector of Dublin, 1659. [CSPIre]

DOBBS, ARTHUR, at the Surveyor General's Office in Dublin, a letter, 1739. [PRONI.D162.27]

DOBSON, ISAAC, a merchant, son of Isaac Dobson a merchant, was admitted as a Freeman of Dublin in 1672. [DLA]

DOBSON, WILLIAM, a merchant, formerly apprentice of William Quaille a merchant, was admitted as a Freeman of Dublin in 1698. [DLA]

DODD, THOMAS, in Dublin, a letter, 1729. [PRONI.D2707.A1.1.16A]

DODD, Mrs, wife of Mr Dodd a tallow chandler in Marlborough Street, Dublin, died in 1766. [FDJ.4120]

DODSON, JOHN, in Damask Street, St Andrews parish, Dublin, in 1659. [C]

DOGHERTY, ANNE, in Jervais Street, Dublin, married a Mr Jennings in 1764. [FDJ.3833]

DOGOOD, GEORGE, a shoemaker of Queen Street, Dublin, married Alice Savage of Channel Row, Dublin, in 1766. [FDJ.4102]

D'OLIER, THEOPHILIUS, a merchant from Dublin, died in Barbados on 22 November 1809. [Barbados Mercury; 25.11.1809] [St Michael's Cathedral MI, Barbados]

DOMINICK, CHRISTOPHER, in Dublin, a lease, 1680. [PRONI.D366.1]

DONALDSON, ELIZABETH, in Dublin, a will, 1773. [PRONI.T700.1]

DONGAN, JOHN, son and heir of William Dongan late of Dublin, 1627. [CSPIre]

DONNOLLY, PETER, born 1787, a clerk in Dublin, emigrated aboard the Rover of New York, master George Bray, bound for New York in 1805. [BM.Addl.ms35762,103]

DORAN, PATRICK, master of the Owner's Goodwill of Dublin bound to Madeira and the West Indies in 1723. [NLI.ma14.165]

DORES, WILLIAM, in Chequer Lane, Dublin, in 1659. [C]

DOUGLAS, ROBERT, in Dublin, 1663. [PRONI.D1618.15.2.33]

DOWDA, EDWARD, in Dublin, a post nuptial marriage settlement of Roger Bamber and Teresa, daughter of Edward Dowda, 1652. [PRONI.D514.1]

DOWDALL, Captain GEORGE, a Roman Catholic officer in Dublin, 1693. [Cal.SPDom.1693.16]

DOWDALL, Captain JOHN, a Roman Catholic officer in Dublin, 1693. [Cal.SPDom.1693.16]

DOWDALL, Ensign JOHN, a Roman Catholic officer in Dublin, 1693. [Cal.SPDom.1693.16]

DOWDALL, JOHN, a joiner and a brother of the Corporation of Carpenters in Dublin, 1656. [DCA.G2/1]

DOWLE, WILLIAM, a merchant in Dublin, 1611. [Carew ms]; {?} a baker, was admitted as a Freeman of Dublin in 1615.[DLA]

DOWLEY, MARCUS, in Dublin, will, 1754, refers to his wife Abigail Wolfinder, his eldest daughter Ann, wife of Archdeacon Daniel Hearn; wits. Patrick Dunn an attorney at the Court of the King's Bench in Ireland, Thomas Quin an apothecary in Dublin, Marlborough Sterling the Deputy Protonotary of the Court of Common Pleas in Ireland, and Archdeacon Daniel Hearn. [DRD]

DOWLIN, PATRICK, a mariner and privateer of Dublin, 1756-1796. [MM.97.49-66]

DOWLING, JOHN, a cooper and a member of the Fraternity of St Patrick's near Dublin in 1666. [CSPIre]

DOWLING, JOHN, son of John Dowling a timber merchant in Back Lane, Dublin, died in Jamaica in 1765. [FDJ.23.4.1765]

DOWLING, PATRICK, a carpenter and a brother of the Corporation of Carpenters in Dublin, 1656. [DCA.G2/1]

DOWLING, ..., a timber merchant in Back Lane, Dublin, married Mrs Dawson, a widow, of Blind Quay, Dublin, in 1766. [FDJ.4108]

DOWNES, ROBERT, in Dublin, will, 1754, refers to his wife Elizabeth, wits. William Dixon NP in Dublin, James White clerk to Edward Sterling, and Edward Sterling NP in Dublin. [DRD]

DOWNY, POLLY, of Hammond Lane, Dublin, married Nicholas Nowlan a distiller in 1764. [FDJ.3928]

DOYLE, THOMAS, born 1767, a planter from Dublin, was naturalised in South Carolina in 1813. [NARA.M1183]

DOYNE, GEORGE, in Dublin, a deed, 1660. [PRONI.D577.3]

DRAYTON, JAMES, a carpenter, was admitted as a Freeman of Dublin in 1651, [DLA]; a carpenter and a brother of the Corporation of Carpenters in Dublin, 1656. [DCA.G2/1]

DRENNAN, Dr WILLIAM, in Dublin, a letter, 1800. [PRONI.D456.13]

DRUMGOLD, JOHN, a Methodist in Dublin, died 1792.

DRURY, SAMUEL, in Damask Street, St Andrews parish, Dublin, in 1659. [C]

DU FAY, D'EXOUDUN, JOSUE, born 1672 in Niort, Poitou, France, a Huguenot soldier in the service of King William, died in Dublin in 1730, buried in Peter Street. [HSP.XLI.37]

DUCROS, JEAN PIERRE, a Huguenot soldier in the service of King William, died 1723 in Dublin. [HSP.XLI.34]

DUFF, EDMOND in Fishamble Street, St John's parish, Dublin, in 1659. [C]

DUFF, MARGARET, daughter of Michael Duff, died on the Strand, Dublin, in 1764. [FDJ.3804]

DUFFIN, C., in Dublin, a letter, 1805. [PRONI.D562.6006]

DUNLOP, ANDREW, a merchant in Dublin, was admitted as a burgess and guilds-brother of Ayr in 1723. [ABR]

DUNLOP, JOHN, in Dublin, a charter party re a voyage from Dublin to Stockholm, Sweden, in 1726. [PRONI.D354.389]

DUNNE, THOMAS, a plasterer and a brother of the Corporation of Carpenters in Dublin, 1656. [DCA.G2/1]

DU PUY, SAMUEL, born around 1655, a Huguenot soldier in the service of King William, died 1707 in Dublin. [HSP.XLI.35]

DU QUERY, Miss, daughter of Mr Du Query a merchant in Dublin, died in 1766. [FDJ.4076]

DU RANG, Mrs ANN, died in 1765, 'she left £30 to the French church in Peter Street, [Dublin]', [FDJ.4052]

DU TORAL, ALEXANDRE BARDEL, a Huguenot soldier in the service of King William, died in Dublin in 1714. [HSP.XLI.68]

DUTTON, JOHN, died in High Street, Dublin, in 1770. [FLJ.53]

DU VAL, AUGUSTE, of Alencon, France, a Huguenot soldier in the service of King William. Died 1719 in Dublin, buried in St Patrick's. [HSP.XLI.35]

DUVALL, LEWIS, formerly manager of Smock Alley Theatre, died in Henry Street, Dublin, in 1766. [FDJ.4075]

DUVALL, Mrs, wife of Mr Duvall late manager of the theatres in Aungier Street and Smock Alley, Dublin, died in 1766. [FDJ.4053]

DWYER, WILLIAM, a fencing master in Dublin, died in County Tipperary in 1766. [FDJ.4103]

DYLLON, GEORGE, of Killeagh, Dublin, 1611. [Carew ms]

EARLE, EDMOND, a distiller, was admitted as a Freeman of Dublin in 1655, [DLA]; a distiller and a brother of the Corporation of Carpenters in Dublin, 1656. [DCA.G2/1]

EARLY, Captain, in St Bride's parish, Dublin, in 1659. [C]

EASTWOOD, GEORGE, a mariner from Dublin, died in Gambia, probate 1688 PCC

EATON, Mr, formerly a goldsmith in Skinner Row, Dublin, died in Dorset Street, Dublin, in 1764. [FDJ.3825]

EATON, Mrs, wife of Mr Eaton of the Customs House in Dublin, died in 1766. [FDJ.4047]

ECCLESTON, TRISTRAM, former Constable of Dublin Castle, 1611. [CSPIre]

ECHLIN, HENRY, in Dublin, a deed, 1680. [PRONI.D69.1]

EDGEWORTH, ROBERT, in Dublin, a will, 1773, refers to his brother Usher, John Usher in County Wicklow, Christopher Usher in County Carlow, wits. Richard Williams a jeweller, Love Theophilus Casson a gentleman, William Williams a notary public, and William Glascock a gentleman, all in Dublin. [DRD]

EDGEWORTH, ..., son of Francis White Edgeworth, was born in Digges Street, Dublin, in 1770. [FLJ.52]

EDKINS, JAMES, in Skinner Row, parish of St Nicholas within the Walls, Dublin, in 1659. [C]

EDMONSTON, ABRAHAM, married Miss Plunket, both of High Street, Dublin, in 1766. [FDJ.4102]

EDWARDS. RICHARD, a gentleman in Trinity Lane, College Green, Dublin, in 1659. [C]

EGAN, BARNABY, a merchant of the Inns Quay, Dublin, married Mary Anne Berne of Thomas Street, Dublin, in 1764. [FDJ.3789]

EGAN, PHILIP, from Dublin, an indentured servant in Philadelphia, 1745. [EP.55]

ELLIOT, CHARLES, from Dublin, an indentured servant bound for Jamaica in 1685. [BRO]

ELLIS, EDWARD, in Dublin, a will, 1773, refers to his wife Mary, son Edward, and grandson Francis Edward Ellis, brother in law Francis Whyte and his daughter Maria, Francis Edgworth in Dublin, Reverend Singleton Harpur in Dublin; wits. Joseph Ellis and John Ellis both cabinetmakers in Dublin, Alexanderson a gentleman in Dublin, and Joseph Griffith a gentleman in Dublin. [DRD]

ELLIS, JOHN, a plasterer, was admitted as a Freeman of Dublin in 1654, [DLA]; a plasterer and a brother of the Corporation of Carpenters in Dublin, 1656. [DCA.G2/1]

ELLIS, THOMAS, a blacksmith, was admitted as a Freeman of Dublin in 1655, [DLA]; a bricklayer and a brother of the Corporation of Carpenters in Dublin, 1656. [DCA.G2/1]

ELLISON, JOHN, a junior Fellow of Trinity College, Dublin, 1771. [CHOP.1771.1006]

ELWARD, ..., a gentleman in Damask Street, St Andrews parish, Dublin, in 1659. [C]

EMERSON, JAMES, master of the Ruby of Dublin trading with Grenada in 1764. [TNA.CO106.1]

ENFANT, ALEXANDRE DAVID, a Huguenot soldier in the service of King William, died in Dublin, 1734. [HSP.XLI.36]

EPWELL, Mrs, widow of Rev. Samuel Epwell and sister of Colonel Edward Corker, died in Princes Street, Dublin, in 1764. [FDJ.3841]

ESPERANDIEU, HENRI D', a Huguenot soldier in the service of King William, died in Dublin in 1703 and buried in St Patrick's. [HSP.XLI.36]

ETON, THEOPHILUS, in Skinner Row, parish of St Nicholas within the Walls, Dublin, in 1659. [C]

EUSTACE, Captain ALEXANDER, a Roman Catholic officer in Dublin in 1693. [CSPIre]

EUSTACE, Colonel, a Roman Catholic officer in Dublin in 1693. [CSPIre]

EVANS, ROBERT, a persecuted Quaker in Dublin, who petitioned King Charles II in 1660. [CSPIre]

EVANS, Mrs, a widow and a chandler, died in Francis Street, Dublin, in 1764. [FDJ.3831]

EVER, WILLIAM, from Hereford, England, settled in Dublin in 1651, denizised in Ireland during 1662. [IPR]

EVERARD, Captain PATRICK, a Roman Catholic officer in Dublin in 1693. [CSPIre]

EVERS, WILLIAM, in Skinner Row, parish of St Nicholas within the Walls, Dublin, in 1659. [C]

EWING, JOHN, born 1775, a student at Trinity College, Dublin, in 1791, son of Robert Ewing a merchant in Barbados. [AD]

EXSHAW, Mrs, wife of John Exshaw a bookseller in Dame Street, Dublin, died in 1764. [FDJ.3839]

FADE, JAMES, a carpenter, was admitted as a Freeman of Dublin in 1653, [DLA]; a carpenter and a brother of the Corporation of Carpenters in Dublin, 1656. [DCA.G2/1]

FAGAN, CHARLES, a merchant, was admitted as a Freeman of Dublin in 1710. [DLA]

FAGAN, JOHN, a surgeon, was admitted as a Freeman of Dublin in 1750. [DLA]

FAGAN, ..., born 1688, a widow, died in James's Street, Dublin, in 1763. [FDJ.3725]

FANNING, JAMES, married the widow Grace in Dublin, 1764. [FDJ.3820]

FANNING, JOHN, a carpenter, was admitted as a Freeman of Dublin in 1600. [DLA]

FANNING, RICHARD, a baker, was admitted as a Freeman of Dublin in 1673. [DLA]

FARANGE, GABRIEL, born 1660 in Montpellier, France, a Huguenot soldier in the service of King William, died 1730 in Dublin and buried in Peter Street. [HSP.XLI.36]

FARJON, DAVID, born in Nismes, France, a Huguenot soldier in the service of King William, died in Dublin in 1726 and was buried in St Patrick's. [HSP.XLI.36]

FARLEY, RICHARD, in Dublin, a lease, 1670. [PRONI.D430.195]

FARRELL, IGNATIUS, a wigmaker in Dublin, will, 1747, execs. John Mahon his brother-in-law and Paul Mahon, merchants in Dublin, wits Luke Armstrong victualler, Thomas Robertson butcher, Paul Currin, Robert Stafford, all in Dublin. [DRD]

FARRELL, ROBERT, a weaver in New Street, Dublin, was admitted as a Freeman of Dublin in 1762. [DLA]

FARRELL, Lieutenant TERENCE, a Roman Catholic officer in Dublin in 1693. [CSPIre]

FARRELL, THOMAS, from Dublin, an indentured servant bound for America in 1697. [LRO]

FARRELL, THOMAS, a merchant, son of Thomas Farrell, was admitted as a Freeman of Dublin in 1718. [DLA]

FARRELL, Mrs, wife of Mr Farrell a publican, died in Dame Street, Dublin, in 1770. [FLJ.51]

FAULKNER, WILLIAM, a bricklayer and a brother of the Corporation of Carpenters in Dublin, 1656. [DCA.G2/1]

FAULKNER, WILLIAM, a merchant, was admitted as a Freeman of Dublin in 1769. [DLA]

FAULKNER, Mrs, relict of Mr Faulkner a mercer, died in Dame Street, Dublin, in 1764. [FDJ.3925]

FENLON, PATRICK, of Aungier Street, Dublin, an Upholder, married Mary Troy of Smithfield, in 1766. [FDJ.4104]

FENNELL, GERALD, from Dublin, a student at Rheims University in 1614. [RCPE]

FENNELL, ROBERT, a cooper, was admitted as a Freeman of Dublin in 1747. [DLA]

FENNER, RICHARD, a gentleman in Dublin, a lease, 1698. [PRONI.D3007.A13.1]; a barber-surgeon, was admitted as a Freeman of Dublin in 1698. [DLA]

FENTON, Mrs, died in William Street, Dublin, in 1764. [FDJ.3809]

FIELD, Mr, a stone cutter, died in Britain Street, Dublin, in 1764. [FDJ.3806]

FINCH, CHRISTOPHER, born 1592, a skipper in Dublin, a witness before the High Court of the Admiralty of England in 1643. [TNA.HCA13.58.510]

FISHER, HENRY, in Dublin, 1628. [CPRI]

FITZGERALD, EDWARD, a weaver, apprentice to Lott Rhodes, was admitted as a Freeman of Dublin in 1703. [DLA]

FITZGERALD, GEORGE, a tallow chandler, son of Timothy Fitzgerald, was admitted as a Freeman of Dublin in 1767. [DLA]

FITZGERALD, JOHN, a gentleman in Wine Tavern Street, Dublin, 1659. [C]

FITZGERALD, JOSEPH, a cooper in Temple Bar, Dublin, apprentice to Anthony Allen, was admitted as a Freeman of Dublin in 1742. [DLA]

FITZGERALD, Colonel MAURICE, a Roman Catholic officer in Dublin in 1693. [CSPIre]

FITZGERALD, RICHARD, in Dublin, 1632. [IPR.607]

FITZGERALD, Captain, a Roman Catholic officer in Dublin in 1693. [CSPIre]

FITZGERALD, ..., master of the Society of Dublin trading with Philadelphia and the West Indies in 1712. [APCCol.iv.244]

FITZHARRIS, Captain EDWARD, a Roman Catholic officer in Dublin in 1693. [CSPIre]

FITZHARRIS, JOHN, a merchant, was admitted as a Freeman of Dublin in 1630. [DLA]

FITZHARRIS, RICHARD, a merchant, was admitted as a Freeman of Dublin in 1626. [DLA]

FITZSYMON, CHRISTOPHER, a merchant in Dublin, husband of Barbara White, a will, 1710. [DRD]

FITZSIMMONS, NICHOLAS, in High Street, Dublin, in 1626. [CSPIre]

FITZSIMMONS, MARY, and Thomas Taylor, in Dublin, a marriage contract, 1604. [PRONI.D430.110]

FITZWILLIAMS, Lord OLIVER, in Irishtown, Dublin, in 1659. [C]

FITZWILLIAM, Sir THOMAS, of Meryouge, Dublin, 1611. [Carew mss]

FITZWILLIAMS, WILLIAM, in Irishtown, Dublin, 1659. [C]

FLACK, JAMES, a baker, was admitted as a Freeman of Dublin in 1723. [DLA]; in Dublin, a letter, 1766. [PRONI.D2707.A1.1.77]

FLEMINGE, Captain MICHAEL, a Roman Catholic officer in Dublin in 1693. [CSPIre]

FLEMING, ROBERT, a glover, son of George Fleming, was admitted as a Freeman of Dublin in 1742. [DLA]

FLETCHER, JOHN, from Lawtonhope, Hertfordshire, died in Dublin, probate 1696, PCC

FLETCHER, LAURENCE, a felt-maker, was admitted as a Freeman of Dublin in 1668. [DLA]

FLETCHER, ROBERT, a merchant, son of James Fletcher, was admitted as a Freeman of Dublin in 1694. [DLA]

FLETCHER, SUSAN, widow of Peter Fletcher in Dublin, a deed, 1698. [PRONI.D645.5]

FLETCHER, Mrs, wife of Dr Fletcher, died in Stephen Street, Dublin, in 1766. [FDJ.4060]

FLINN, BARNABY, a dyer in Meath Street, Dublin, apprentice to George Newland, was admitted as a Freeman of Dublin in 1762. [DLA]

FLINN, PATRICK, a dealer in Cavensport, Dublin, will, 1753, wife Margaret Flinn, daughters Bridget and Martha, wits. Joseph Greason a shoemaker, William Bryan a dairyman, and Robert McMullen a gentleman in Dublin. [DRD]

FLINN, THOMAS, a bricklayer, was admitted as a Freeman of Dublin in 1735. [DLA]

FLIN, ..., daughter of Mr Flin a bookseller in Dublin, died in 1766. [FDJ.4111]

FLINT, BENJAMIN, a tape weaver, was admitted as a Freeman of Dublin in 1772. [DLA]

FLINT, JOHN, a merchant in Dublin, Pursuivant of HM Court of the Exchequer in Ireland from 1609. [HMC.35]

FLOOD, ALICE, a spinster, was admitted as a Freeman of Dublin in 1713. [DLA]

FLOOD, HENRY, a merchant, was admitted as a Freeman of Dublin in 1771. [DLA]

FLOOD, JOHN, a vintner of Summer Hill, Dublin, married Nancy Harris of Skinner's Alley on the Combe, in 1766. [FDJ.4120]

FLOODGATE, Ensign THOMAS, a Roman Catholic officer in Dublin in 1693. [CSPIre]

FLOYD, THOMAS, in Skinner Row, parish of St Nicholas within the Walls, Dublin, in 1659. [C]

FLOWER, HENRY, and his wife Anne ..... in Dublin, a lease, 1677. [PRONI.D6.1]; a weaver, a Quaker, was admitted as a Freeman of Dublin in 1695. [DLA]

FLOWER, TURVEY, son of Mark Flower, a pin maker, died in Pill Lane, Dublin, in 1764. [FDJ.3924]

FLOYD, JOHN, a scholar at Trinity College, Dublin, in 1618. [CSPIre]

FOGARTY, ..., a distiller, died on Merchant's Quay, Dublin, in 1766. [FDJ.4108]

FOLEY, PATRICK, of Pill Lane, Dublin, married Miss Dempsey of Mary Street, Dublin, in 1764. [FDJ.3924]

FOLLET, JOHN, in Dublin, a letter, 1691. [PRONI.D429.37]

FOORTH, ROBERT, in Dublin, son of the late Sir Ambrose Foorth, 1627, [CSPIre]

FORBES, JOHN, a merchant, was admitted as a Freeman of Dublin in 1723. [DLA]; in Dublin, a charter party re a voyage from Dublin to Stockholm, Sweden, in 1726. [PRONI.D354.389]

FORBES, SAMUEL, a doctor of physics in Dublin, testament 1724, Commissariat of Edinburgh. [NRS]

FORDE, ARTHUR, Surveyor of the Customs House Quay, Dublin, died in 1766, [FDJ.4057]

FORREST, THOMAS, a wheelwright, was admitted as a Freeman of Dublin in 1719. [DLA]

FORREST, THOMAS, a merchant in Dublin, was admitted as a burgess and guilds-brother of Glasgow in 1723. [GBR]

FORSTER, EDWARD, a lease of a tenement in Mary Lane, Dublin, 1635. [PRONI.D430.141]

FORSTER, JOHN, a gentleman from Westminster, died in Dublin, probate 1690, PCC.

FORTANIER, DANIEL, a Huguenot soldier in the service of King William, died in Dublin in 1726, buried in Peter Street. [HSP.XLI.38]

FOSTER, ANTHONY, in Dublin, an agreement, 1736. [PRONI.D207.3.1]

FOSTER, JOHN, in Dublin, a letter, 1781. [PRONI.D207.67.3]

FOSTER, Reverend WILLIAM, in Dublin, 1787. [PRONI.D207.19.1573]

FOULIS, THOMAS, in St Bride's parish, Dublin, in 1659. [C]

FOUNBAINE, JAMES. in Sheep Street, St Bride's parish, Dublin, 1659. [C]

FOWKE, JANE, a spinster in London, later in St Nicholas without the walls, Dublin, probate 1682 PCC

FOWNES, W., in Dublin, a letter, 1692. [PRONI.D429.55]

FOX, JOHN, a cutler, was admitted as a Freeman of Dublin in 1664, [DLA]; a cutler and a member of the Guild of St Luke the Evangelist in Dublin, 1669. [CSPIre]

FOXWICH, SAMUEL, in Chequer Lane, Dublin, in 1659. [C]

FRANCIS, JAMES, a Swiss, naturalised in Dublin, 1794. [NRAS.3955.60.2.132]

FRANCKE, JOHN, a printer in Dublin, 1602. [SPI.1602.410]

FRANKS, THOMAS THORPE, in Suffolk Street, Dublin, a letter, 1810. [PRONI.D562.9690]

FRANKLIN, Captain JOHN, in Damask Street, St Andrews parish, Dublin, in 1659. [C]

FREEMAN, THOMAS, born 1626, a merchant in Dublin, a witness before the High Court of the Admiralty of England in 1646. [TNA.HCA1.59.701]; a merchant, was admitted as a Freeman of Dublin in 1652. [DLA]

FREEMAN, THOMAS, a cooper and a brother of the Corporation of Carpenters in Dublin, 1656. [DCA.G2/1]; a cooper and a member of the Fraternity of St Patrick's near Dublin in 1666. [CSPIre]

FRENCH, Captain ARTHUR, a Roman Catholic officer in Dublin in 1693. [CSPIre]

FRENCH, HUMPHREY, a merchant, was admitted as a Freeman of Dublin in 1769. [DLA]

FRENCH, MATTHEW, a merchant, son of Richard French, was admitted as a Freeman of Dublin in 1769. [DLA]

FRENCH, NICHOLAS, an 'ale draper' in Dublin, will 1750, wife Alice French, nieces Elizabeth, Catherine, and Margaret, wits. Captain Michael Reilly, Richard Keen, Henry Stevens Reilly, all in Dublin. [DRD]

FRENCH, PATRICK, formerly in Dublin, later in Duras, County Galway, a Roman Catholic licenced to bear arms in 1705. [HMC.Ormonde.ii.476]; died 1708, will. [DRD]

FRENCH, R.H., a merchant in Dublin, a petition, 1800. [PRONI.D207.23.40]

FRENCH, THOMAS, master of the Minerva of Dublin trading with Spain in 1705. [Cal.SP.Dom.SP44.393.75]

FRENCH, Miss, of Blind Quay, Dublin, married Dennis Kelly an attorney, in 1764. [FDJ.3832]

FRYE, JOHN, in Dublin, a deposition, 1641. [PRONI.D1923.1.14.AV]

FULLAM, DENIS, a joiner and a brother of the Corporation of Carpenters in Dublin, 1656. [DCA.G2/1]

FULLER, GEORGE, a weaver in Francis Street, Dublin, son of Nicholas Fuller, was admitted as a Freeman of Dublin in 1740 [DLA]

FULLER, JACOB, a Quaker merchant, was admitted as a Freeman of Dublin in 1691. [DLA]

FULLER, JOSEPH, jr, in Thomas Court, Dublin, will, 1766, refers to his brothers Abraham and John, also Joseph Thomas Fuller son of the said Abraham; wits. Luke Reilly a hatter in Thomas Court, Dublin, Thomas Bewley jr a grocer in Clare Street, Dublin, Thomas Reilly servant to Joseph Fuller, and Samuel Hatch clerk to Adam Williams in Dublin. [DRD]

FURLONG, Captain JAMES, in Dublin, a Roman Catholic licenced to bear arms in 1705. [HMC.Ormonde.ii.476]

FURY, GEORGE, a felt-maker, apprentice of John Fury, was admitted as a Freeman of Dublin in 1769. [DLA]

FURY, Captain JOHN, a Roman Catholic officer in Dublin in 1693. [CSPIre]

GAINSFORD, Captain FRANCIS, in Dublin, probate 1614 PCC

GALBRAITH, JAMES, in Dublin, letters, 1800. [PRONI.D623A.92.35]; was admitted as a Freeman of Dublin in 1816. [DLA]

GALBRAITH, MARK ANTHONY, married Miss Barbara Davison, in Dublin in 1766. [FDJ.4063]

GALBRAITH, ROSE, in Dublin, a will, 1758. [PRONI.T700.1]

GAMBLE, HANS, formerly in Dublin, died in Mullingar in 1766. [FDJ.4083]

GAMBLE, HENRY, a mason, was admitted as a Freeman of Dublin in 1651. [DLA]; a mason and a brother of the Corporation of Carpenters in Dublin, 1656. [DCA.G2/1]

GANNON, JAMES, died in Marshal Alley, Coal Quay, Dublin, in 1766. [FDJ.4081]

GANRING, BRYAN, born 1686, an indentured servant aboard the Providence of Dublin landed in Middlesex County, Virginia, in 1699. [WI.194]

GARDINER, GEORGE, Controller of the Stores in the Customs House in Dublin, died in 1765. [FDJ.3932]

GARDINER, ..., a dentist in Cow Lane, Dublin, died of a duelling wound in 1764. [FDJ.3789]

GARDNER, ..., in Dublin, and his lady, Elizabeth, Countess of Kilmarnock, testament, 1712, Commissariat of Edinburgh. [NRS]

GARLAND, JOHN, a cooper, was admitted as a Freeman of Dublin in 1654. [DLA]; a cooper and a brother of the Corporation of Carpenters in Dublin, 1656. [DCA.G2/1]

GARLAND, JOHN, a cooper and a member of the Fraternity of St Patrick's near Dublin in 1666. [CSPIre]

GAVAN, MICHAEL, born 1747, married Miss Ann Dardis of Francis Street, Dublin, born 1675, in 1766. [FDJ.4112]

GAVAN, WALTER, a surgeon in Dublin, died aboard HMS Bredah probate 1698, PCC

GAVAN, Mrs, wife of William Gavan, died on the Bachelor's Walk, Dublin, in 1766. [FDJ.4061]

GAY, Captain JOHN, in St George's Lane, Dublin, letters to William Penn in 1669. [CSPIre]

GAYNOR, JOHN, a mariner in Cole Alley, Meath Street, Dublin, his wife Mary Collins, his daughters Catherine and Ann Gaynor; wits. Martin Fitzgerald a carpenter in Dublin, Edward Biker a weaver in Dublin, and John Callaghan a gentleman in Dublin. [DRD]

GAYNOR, ..., a chicken butcher in the Castle Market, Dublin, died in 1764. [FDJ.3841]

GEALE, FREDERICK, in Dublin, a letter, 1800. [PRONI.D562.14826]

GEESON, Mrs, sister of Mrs Fitzhenry, died at the Back of Blind Quay, Dublin, in 1766. [FDJ.4125]

GENISON, THOMAS, in Dublin, probate 1587, PCC

GEOGHEGAN, Major WILLIAM, in Dublin, a Roman Catholic licenced to bear arms, 1705. [HMC.Ormond.ii.476]

GEORGE, WILLIAM, a glover, was admitted as a Freeman of Dublin in 1672, [DLA]; a skinner in Dublin, probate 1687, PCC

GERNON, PATRICK, a carpenter, died at his house in Ormond Market, Dublin, in 1766. [FDJ.4077]

GERRARD, JAMES, a baker in Thomas Street, Dublin, married the widow Byrne of Dundalk, in 1766. [FDJ.4101]

GERRARD, or MASON, MARY, a widow in Dublin, will, 1750, her son Mason Gerrard, her daughters Barbara, wife of Henry Marsh, and Sarah, wife of John Burton, niece Elizabeth Jenkins, John Nixon a clothier, and John Ross an apothecary; wits. Benjamin Johnston NP, and his clerk Richard Thwaites, Anthony Hart servant to John Burton, and William Hall, all in Dublin. [DRD]

GERRARD, PETER, master of the Eagle of Dublin trading with Bilbao, Spain, in 1705. [CalSPDom.SP44.392.72]

GEYLENSON, MEYLES, from Zealand, a resident of Dublin, denizised in Ireland in 1622. [IPR]

GIBBONS, CHRISTOPHER, in Dublin, a lease, 1606. [PRONI.D430.112]

GIBBONS, Mrs, wife of Andrew Gibbons a baker in Poolbeg Street, Dublin, died in 1766. [FDJ.4099]

GIBERNE, JEAN, of St Hippolyte, Languedoc, France, a Huguenot soldier in the service of King William, died 1737 in Dublin. [HSP.XLI.41]

GIBSON, WILLIAM, a carpenter, was admitted as a Freeman of Dublin in 1747, [DLA]; a cabinet maker in Dublin, will, 1758, refers to his wife Jane Curry, his father-in-law John Curry, his sister-in-law Elizabeth Curry, his nephews William Mooney and Antony Mooney; wits. James McFann a carrier, Thomas Green a silversmith, William Wilkinson a joiner, and William Dixon NP, all of Dublin. [DRD]

GIBTON, JOHN, of Great Butter Lane, Dublin, married Anne Poole of Blackpitts, in 1765. [FDJ.3935]

GILBERT, GEORGE, born 1611, a merchant in Dublin, a witness before the High Court of the Admiralty of England in 1647, [TNA.HCA13.59.518]; in Dublin, a deed, 1656. [PRONI.D430.158]

GILBERT, ZECHIEL, was admitted as a Freeman of Dublin in 1654, [DLA]; a carpenter and a brother of the Corporation of Carpenters in Dublin, 1656. [DCA.G2/1]

GILES, THOMAS, a cooper and a brother of the Corporation of Carpenters in Dublin, 1656. [DCA.G2/1]

GILL, JOHN, of New Row, Dublin, married Miss Bushell of Francis Street, Dublin, in 1770. [FLJ.50]

GILL, ROBERT, was admitted as a Freeman of Dublin in 1654, [DLA]; a butcher in Dublin, denizised in Ireland during 1667. [IPR]; took the Oath of Allegiance and Supremacy to King Charles II in 1667.

GILL, WILLIAM, master of the brigantine Nancy of Dublin trading with Charleston, South Carolina, and with Barbados in 1735-1737. [TNA.CO5.509-510; CO33.16][SCGaz: 24.5.1735]

GIRARD, PHILIPPE, of Arles, Bouches du Rhone, France, born 1658, a Huguenot soldier in the service of King William, died in Dublin 1730, buried in Peter Street. [HSP.XLI.41]

GIRVAN, JOHN, in Dublin, a letter, 1789. [PRONI.D562.8106]

GLADSTONES, THOMAS, a merchant in Dublin, was admitted as a burgess and guilds-brother of Glasgow in 1724. [GBR]FDJ.4086]

GLASCORD, ROGER, in Sheep Street, St Bride's parish, Dublin, 1659. [C]

GLEADOWE, THOMAS, a banker, died in Castle Street, Dublin, in 1766. [FDJ

GLOVER, Captain, a gentleman in Trinity Lane, College Green, Dublin, in 1659. [C]

GODOLPHIN, FRANCIS, Principal Secretary at Dublin Castle, probate 1676 PCC

GOLDIE, EBENEZER, of the Customs in Dublin, was admitted as a burgess and guilds-brother of Ayr in 1786. [ABR]

GOLLIER, JAMES, master of the Rebecca of Dublin bound for the West Indies in 1642. [NRS.RD1.544.6]

GOOD, THOMAS, in Dublin, a deed re the house Nampatuck, High Street, Dublin, 1670. [PRONI.T1706.1]

GOODACRE, GIDEON, born 1677, former apprentice to Robert Prosser, was admitted as a Freeman of Dublin in 1763, [DLA]; a glover in Pill Lane, Dublin, died in 1765. [FDJ.3934]

GOODAKER, JOHN, a joiner was admitted as a Freeman of Dublin in 1650, DLA]; and a brother of the Corporation of Carpenters in Dublin, 1656. [DCA.G2/1]

GOODBODY, Mrs ELEANOR, wife of Samuel Goodbody a merchant in Dublin, died in 1764. [FDJ.3833]

GOODYEAR, ANNE, widow of Thomas Kennedy in Dublin, died in London, probate 1691 PCC

GORDON, ALEXANDER, a Captain of the Royal Regiment of Foot, late in Dublin, testament, 1733, Commissariat of Edinburgh. [NRS]

GORDON, FRANCIS, a butcher, son of Robert Gordon, was admitted as a Freeman of Dublin in 1759. [DLA]; died in Walker's Alley, Dublin, in 1763. [FDJ.3725]

GORDON, Mrs, wife of Charles Gordon, died in Granby Row, Dublin, in 1764. [FDJ.3820]

GORDON, ..., formerly Captain of the Royal Scots Regiment of Foot, died in Marlborough Street, Dublin, in 1766. [FDJ.4076]

THE PEOPLE OF DUBLIN, 1600-1799

GORE, FREDERICK, in Sackville Street, Dublin, died in 1764. [FDJ.3846]

GORMAN, Miss M., from Dublin, died on Madeira in 1810. [ARM]

GOUGE, EDMOND, in Stevens Street, Dublin, 1659. [C]

GOULD, ADAM, a merchant in Wine Tavern Street, Dublin, 1659. [C]

GOULD, JAMES, a gentleman in Wine Tavern Street, Dublin, 1659. [C]

GOVAN, PATRICK, servant to Bryce Blair a merchant in Dublin, was admitted as a burgess and guilds-brother of Ayr in 1734. [ABR]

GOVAN, THOMAS, a tailor in Dublin, was denisized in Ireland during 1669. [IPR]; took the Oath of Allegiance to King Charles II in 1669.

GRATTAN, JAMES, a Representative and Recorder of Dublin, died in Granby Row, Dublin, in 1766. [FDJ.4083]

GRAVES, THOMAS, a member of the Guild of Brewers in Dublin in 1669. [CSPIre]

GRAVES, RICHARD, was admitted to the Merchant Guild of Dublin in 1686. [DGM]

GRAVES, Captain, in Damask Street, St Andrews parish, Dublin, in 1659. [C]

GRAY, Captain JOHN, in Dublin, was admitted as a burgess and guilds-brother of Ayr in 1738. [ABR]

GREEN, HENRY, in Dublin, a letter, 1705. [NRS.CH12,12,365]

GREENE, W., in Dublin, a letter, 1800. [PRONI.D572.8.82]

GREEN, Mrs, wife of Thomas Green a brewer, died in James Street, Dublin, in 1764. [FDJ.3843]

GREENWAY, ROBERT, in Dublin, a letter, 1720. [PRONI.D207.20.18]

GREGG, ANDREW, master of the Providence of Dublin trading with Maryland in 1699. [SPAWI.1699.322]

GREG, HUGH, a merchant in Dublin, was admitted as a burgess and guilds-brother of Glasgow in 1713. [GBR]

GREGG, Mrs, in Michael's Lane, Dublin, died 1766. [FDJ.4080]

GREHAN, EDWARD, a mariner from Dublin, was naturalised in South Carolina in 1798. [NASA.M1183]

GRICE, ANNA, wife of Thomas Parnell a gentleman in Dublin, letters, 1699-1700. [TCD.750.664/694/1705]

GRIERSON, ROBERT, a gentleman in Dublin, a will, 1775, refers to William Hale a silk weaver in Meath Street, Dublin, Richard Hale an ironmonger in Dublin; wits. Mark Bloxham a tallow chandler in Dublin, Festus Kelly a shoemaker in Dublin, Townly Ahmuty a gentleman in Dublin, John Gelling a gentleman in Dublin and his clerk John Scallion. [DRD]

GRIFFIN, WILLIAM, in the Gib Dorsone, Dublin, a lease, 1673. [PRONI.D430.198]

GRIFFITH, WILLIAM, a plasterer, was admitted as a Freeman of Dublin in 1732. [DLA]

GRIFFITH, WILLIAM, master of the Welsh Alehouse in Hawkin's Street, Dublin, died in 1766. [FDJ.4081]

GRIMAUDET, BENJAMIN, born 1663 in Poitiers, France, a Huguenot soldier in the service of King William, died in Dublin 1710. [HSP.XLI.43]

GRIMSDITCH, GEORGE, a former Customs Collector of Dublin, 1611. [CSPIre]

GROSSE, MARTIN, master of the Hare of Dublin which was captured by Parliamentary forces when bound from Dublin to Beaumaris, Wales, in 1644.[TNA.HCA13.62]

GUION, DANIEL, from Charente Inferieux, France, a Huguenot wine merchant in Dublin, died 1733. [HSP.XLI.43]

GUIY, JOHN, a gentleman, in Stevens Street, Dublin, 1659. [C]

GUNNING, JOHN, in Dublin, a letter, 1709. [PRONI.D562.25]

GUTCH, EDWARD, a gentleman in Trinity Lane, College Green, Dublin, in 1659. [C]

HADSEN, NICHOLAS, from Dublin, died aboard the ship Lark, probate 1679, PCC

HALFPENNY, PATRICK, a cooper and a brother of the Corporation of Carpenters in Dublin, 1656. [DCA.G2/1]; a cooper, was admitted as a Freeman of Dublin in 1663. [DLA]

HALGAN, DANIEL, born in Dublin, a glazier, took the Oath of Allegiance and Supremacy to King Charles II in 1671; was admitted as a Freeman of Dublin in 1672. [DLA]

HALGAN, NICHOLAS, a cooper, was admitted as a Freeman of Dublin in 1635, [DLA]; a cooper and a brother of the Corporation of Carpenters in Dublin, 1656. [DCA.G2/1]

HALL, GEORGE, a mariner in Dublin, died at sea aboard the ship Loyal Resolution, probate 1683, PCC

HALL, JAMES, born 1795 in Dublin, naturalised in Charleston, South Carolina, in 1829. [NARA.M1183]

HALL, JEREMIAH, a medical doctor from Halifax, Yorkshire, later in Dublin, probate 1691 PCC

HALL, Reverend Dr JOHN, of Trinity College, Dublin, a bond, 1698. [PRONI.D207.19.14]

HALL, MARGERY, a widow from London, later in Dublin, probate 1675 PCC

HALL, ROBERT, in Chequer Lane, Dublin, in 1659. [C]

HALL, WILLIAM, a merchant in Dublin, dead by 1666. [CSPIre]

HALL, WILLIAM, town major of the garrison in Dublin, 1771. [CHOP.1771.984]

HALL, Mr, a book-binder, died in Coghill's Court, Dame Street, Dublin, in 1764. [FDJ.3814]

HALLORAN, JOHN, master of the Success of Dublin bound for Bilbao, Spain, in 1705. [CalSPDom.SP44.392.66]

HAMILTON, CHARLES, 24 Summerhill, Dublin, a letter, 1793. [PRONI.T2541.1B.3.4.53]

HAMILTON, CLAUDIUS, in Granby Road, Dublin, a letter, 1768. [PRONI.D623A.38.13]

HAMILTON, GALBRAITH, a merchant on Omand Quay, Dublin, was admitted as a Freeman of Dublin in 1759. [DLA]

HAMILTON, JOHN, master of the Providence of Dublin trading with Virginia in 1699. [XJVa.i.458]

HAMILTON, JOHN, a weaver, son of William Hamilton, was admitted as a Freeman of Dublin in 1746.[DLA]

HAMILTON, JOSEPH, a stationer, son of Edward Hamilton, was admitted as a Freeman of Dublin in 1759. [DLA]

HAMILTON, MARLBOROUGH STIRLING, born 1756, a schoolmaster from Dublin, naturalised in Charleston, South Carolina, in 1813. [NARA.M1183]

HAMILTON, ROBERT, was admitted to the Merchant Guild of Dublin in 1604. [DGM]

HAMILTON, WILLIAM, in Dublin, a deed, 1694. [PRONI.D74.1]

HAMILTON, S., in Dublin Castle, a letter, 1789. [PRONI.D562.8076]

HAMILTON, Miss, of Granby Row, Dublin, married Reverend Dr Preston in 1764. [FDJ.3809]

HAMOND, EDWARD, in Dublin, Roman Catholic who was licenced to bear arms in 1705. [HMC.Ormond.ii.476]

HAMMOND, ELIZABETH, a spinster in Dublin, probate 1673 PCC

HANBIDGE, HENRY, a silk thrower in Fishamble Street, Dublin, died in 1764. [FDJ.3829]

HANKISON, RICHARD, in Dublin, will, 1751, daughter Margaret Cochran, Mrs Mary Stapleton; wits. Abel Onge, William Dixon NP, and Thomas Dixon a hosier, all in Dublin. [DRD]

HANRAN, PATRICK, a bricklayer and a brother of the Corporation of Carpenters in Dublin, 1656. [DCA.G2/1]

HANSARD, MARY, a widow in a Dublin suburb, a will, 1709. [DRD]

HANWAY, RICHARD, a merchant, was admitted as a Freeman of Dublin in 1666, [DLA]; a member of the Guild of Brewers in Dublin, 1669, [CSPIre]; an alderman of Dublin, probate 1687 PCC

HANWAY, WILLIAM, clerk of the Guild of Brewers in Dublin, 1669. [CSPIre]

HARDING, JOHN, in Dublin, a deposition, 1641. [PRONI.D1923.1.16J]

HARDINGE, PHILIP, a slater, was admitted as a Freeman of Dublin in 1651. [DLA]; a helier and a brother of the Corporation of Carpenters in Dublin, 1656. [DCA.G2/1]

HARDING, ROBERT, and family, in Dublin, 1658. [CSPCol.xiii]

HARPENNY, PATRICK, a cooper and a member of the Fraternity of St Patrick's near Dublin in 1666. [CSPIre]

HARPER, Miss MARY, a miller in Dame Street, Dublin, died 1764. [FDJ.334]

HARPER, Mrs, wife of Mr Harper a linen-draper in the Corn Market, Dublin, died 1766. [FDJ.4043]

HARINGTON, JOHN, in Chequer Lane, Dublin, in 1659. [C]

HARRIS, FRANCIS, in Skinner Row, parish of St Nicholas within the Walls, Dublin, in 1659. [C]

HARRIS, JOHN, born 1606, a merchant in Dublin, a witness before the High Court of the Admiralty of England in 1636, [TNA.HCA13.46.310]

HARRIS, JOHN, from Dublin, settled in Charleston, South Carolina, administration 1804, PCC

HARRIS, PHILLIP, in Skinner Row, parish of St Nicholas within the Walls, Dublin, in 1659. [C]

HARRIS, WALTER, in Dublin, 1689. [NRS.GD26.8.15]

HARRISON, HENRY, in Dublin, a lease, 1773. [PRONI.D1255.4.1.13A]

HARRISON, JOHN, a helier and a brother of the Corporation of Carpenters in Dublin, 1656. [DCA.G2/1]; a joiner, was admitted as a Freeman of Dublin in 1763, [DLA]

HARRISON, JOHN, in Dublin, a lease, 1773. [PRONI.D1255.4.1.13A]

HARRISON, PETER, a bricklayer, was admitted as a Freeman of Dublin in 1630, [DLA]; a bricklayer and a brother of the Corporation of Carpenters in Dublin, 1656. [DCA.G2/1]

HART, ROGER, born 1685, a publican in Fleet Street, Dublin, died in 1766. [FDJ.4041]

HARTFORD, Mr, a linen draper, died in Bride Street, Dublin, in 1764. [FDJ.3820]

HARTFORD, Mr, died in Francis Street, Dublin, in 1764. [FDJ.3927]

HARTLEY, ELIZABETH, of Francis Street, Dublin, married John Giball jr, in 1770. [FLJ.53]

HARTRED, CHRISTOPHER, was admitted as a Freeman of Dublin in 1654, [DLA]; a turner and a brother of the Corporation of Carpenters in Dublin, 1656. [DCA.G2/1]

HAST, PIERCE, a gentleman in Trinity Lane, College Green, Dublin, in 1659. [C]

HATFIELD, RIDGLEY, Mayor of the Staple of the city of Dublin, an indenture, 1658, [PRONI.D1618.1.7]; an Alderman of Dublin in 1659. [CSPIre]; in Skinner Row, parish of St Nicholas within the Walls, Dublin, in 1659. [C]

HAUGHTON, WILLIAM, of Summer Street, Dublin, married Elizabeth Collier of Chambers Street, Dublin, in 1765. [FDJ.3934]

HAVEY, JOHN, from Dublin, an indentured servant in Philadelphia, 1745. [EP.54]

HAWKERIDGE, JOHN, born 1613, a merchant in Dublin, a witness before the High Court of the Admiralty of England in 1637 and 1640. [TNA.HCA13.53.189/55.544]

HAWKINS, WILLIAM, in Thomas Court, Dublin, a lease, 1708. [PRONI.D645.12]

HAWTHORNE, MARGARET, born 1771, in Britain Street, Dublin, with children James Hawthorne, born 1797, and Kitty, born 1800, also their servant Sally born 1786, emigrated aboard the Rover of New York, master George Bray, bound for New York in 1805. [BM.Addl.ms35762.103]

HAY, JOHN, in Dublin, probate 1671 PCC

HAY, Mrs, wife of Edward Hay in Church Street, Dublin, died in 1764. [FDJ.3925]

HAYDON, THOMAS, a gentleman, in Damask Street, St Andrews parish, Dublin, in 1659. [C]

HAYES, GRIFFITH, Porter of Dublin Castle, 1626. [CSPIre]

HAYES, JOHN, born 1615, a merchant in Dublin, a witness before the High Court of the Admiralty of England in 1643. [TNA.HCA13.58.588]

HAYS, JACQUES DE, a Huguenot soldier in the service of King William, died in Dublin 1757. [HSP.XLI.45]

HEATH, RICHARD, the Searcher and Gauger of the Port of Dublin 1626. [CPRIre]

HEATH, WALTER, born 1600, in Dublin, a witness before the High Court of the Admiralty of England in 1643, [TNA.HCA13.]

HELEY, Mrs, wife of Mr Heley a velvet-weaver, died in Wolfe's Alley, Bride Street, Dublin, in 1764. [FDJ.3790]

HELMES, ROBERT, a merchant in Dublin, 1679. [LRS.36.107]

HENBY, HUGH, a victualler in Dublin, a lease, 1706. [PRONI.D236.1]

HENDERSON, GEORGE, a gentleman in Prussia Street, Dublin, a will, 1775, refers to his wife Margaret, Charles Brown a bookbinder in Dublin, Thomas Ewart a bookbinder in Dublin, James Tomlin, Ann Tomlin, David Murray in Edinburgh, Agnes Hill; wits. John Green, a bookbinder in Dublin, John Hill a bookbinder in Dublin, and William Wilson a gentleman in Dublin. [DRD]

HENDRA, JOHN, master of the Adventure of Dublin part of the Parliamentary Guard for Ireland in 1642, 1643. [IWS.152/153][TNA.Adm.18.2.14]

HENDRY, ROBERT, minister of Capel Street Church, Dublin, from 1692 until his death in 1699. [F.7.530]

HENDRIKIN, WILLIAM, a joiner and a brother of the Corporation of Carpenters in Dublin, 1656. [DCA.G2/1]

HENDY, ARTHUR, in Dublin, a lease, 1665. [PRONI.D430.181]

HENDY, KATHERINE, in Dublin, a lease, 1665. [PRONI.D430.181]

HENLY, ROGER, a gentleman in Dublin, probate 1700 PCC

HENRATTIE, OWEN, in Dublin, a deposition, 1641. [PRONI.D1923.1.19D]

HENRY, HUGH, in Dublin, leases, 1720. [PRONI.T810.7/293-294]

HENSALL, RALPH, a turner and a brother of the Corporation of Carpenters in Dublin, 1656. [DCA.G2/1]

HENSHAW, NATHANIEL, a physician in Dublin, later in London, probate 1673 PCC

HERRON, HENRY, born 1777, a merchant in Dublin, emigrated aboard the Rover of New York, master George Bray, bound for New York in 1805. [BM.Addl.ms35762.103]

HEWITT, JAMES, in Dublin, a lease, 1773. [PRONI.D475.2]

HEWETSON, Reverend CHRISTOPHER, Chancellor of Christ's, Presbyter of St Patrick's, Vicar and Archbishop of Dublin, died 1634. [Sword's MI]

HEWETTSON, or HIGGINS, CHRISTIAN, wife of Percival Hunt an Alderman of Dublin, refers to his sons Percival Hunt the younger and John Hunt in Dublin, her son Richard Higgins, her grandsons James Browne and Laurence Paine, her daughter Christian Paine, Robert Robinson a Doctor of Physick in Dublin, Christopher Robinson one of His Majesty's Councillor at law, and James French in Galway; wits. William Marshall, Richard Thwaites, Benjamin Johnston NP, and Mark Whyte in Dublin. [DRD]

HICKY, MARY, in Dublin, a will, 1665. [PRONI.D430.176]

HICKEY, NOAH, a merchant, apprentice to George Young, was admitted as a Freeman of Dublin in 1747. [DLA]; a confectioner in Capel Street, Dublin, died in 1766. [FDJ.4046]

HICKY, WILLIAM, in Dublin, and his wife Mary Hicky alias Taylor alias Jans, a deed, 1663. [PRONI.D430.160]

HIGGINS, FRANCIS, of the Dublin Customs House, and Ann Gore of Stephen's Green, Dublin, married in 1766. [FDJ.4122]

HILL, ARTHUR, in Dublin, a letter, 1725. [PRONI.D778.61]

HILL, EDWARD, Major of the Artillery in Dublin, husband of Catherine Cartwright, 1743. [NRS.Services of Heirs]

HILL, GEORGE FITZGERALD, in Dublin, letters, 1795, 1800. [PRONI.T2541.1B.3.5.15; D623A.158.3]

HILL, THOMAS, a craner and packer at the port of Dublin in 1625. [CPRIre]

HOARE, JOHN, was admitted as a Freeman of Dublin in 1623. [DLA]; a cooper and a brother of the Corporation of Carpenters in Dublin, 1656. [DCA.G2/1]

HOBART, ROBERT, in Dublin, a lease, 1786. [PRONI.D236.75]

HODGES, HUMPHREY, in Dublin, probate 1681 PCC

THE PEOPLE OF DUBLIN, 1600-1799

HOEY, HANNAH, a widow in Dublin, will, 1773, refers to her grand-daughter Elizabeth Sandys or Ryves, wife of Nehemiah Sandys, Mrs Ann Mills, wits. John Thewless in Dublin, Samuel Paterson in Dublin, William Short a gentleman in Dublin, and Hugh Bernes a gentleman in Dublin. [DRD]

HOGAN, Master JOHN STACKPOLE, died in Cavendish Street, Dublin, in 1766. [FDJ.4067]

HOGHLAN, JOHN, a joiner, was admitted as a Freeman of Dublin in 1655, [DLA]; a joiner and a brother of the Corporation of Carpenters in Dublin, 1656. [DCA.G2/1]

HOLFORD, THOMAS, in Chequer Lane, Dublin, in 1659. [C]

HOLFORD, WILLIAM, in Chequer Lane, Dublin, in 1659. [C]

HOLMES, ROBERT, master of the Fortune of Dublin 1696. [SPAWI.1698.431iv]

HOLMS, ROBERT, a watchmaker in Dublin, was admitted as a Freeman of Belfast in 1730. [TBB]

HOLT, SAMUEL, in Dublin, a deed, 1693. [NAI.2000.20.4.7i/ii]

HOOKE, THOMAS, an alderman of Dublin in 1656. [IC.II.837]; in Skinner Row, parish of St Nicholas within the Walls, Dublin, in 1659. [C]

HOOLE, JAMES, in Dublin, a deposition, 1641. [PRONI.D1923.1.14.AC]

HOOTON, JOHN, a carpenter, was admitted as a Freeman of Dublin in 1653. [DLA]; a carpenter and a brother of the Corporation of Carpenters in Dublin, 1656. [DCA.G2/1]

HOPKINS, ROBERT, a goldsmith, was admitted as a Freeman of Dublin in 1749, [DLA]; died on Ormond Quay, Dublin, in 1766. [FDJ.4141]

HORAGHAN, NICHOLAS, a grocer in Patrick Street, Dublin, died in 1764. [FDJ.3928]

HORE, LUKE, co-owner of the Arran of Dublin which was seized by the Governor of Malaga in Spain in 1684. [CSPDom.1684.204]

HORNER, JOHN, jr., died in Mary's Lane, Dublin, in 1764. [FDJ.3826]

HORISH, JOHN, died in Inn's Quay, Dublin, died in 1766. [FDJ.4046]

HOSKINS, ROBERT, was admitted as a Freeman of Dublin in 1655, [DLA]; a bricklayer and a brother of the Corporation of Carpenters in Dublin, 1656. [DCA.G2/1]

HOUGHTON, MATTHEW, in Dublin, a bill of exchange, 1733. [PRONI.D354.419]

HOUSTON, Mrs, died in Cow Lane, Dublin, in 1770. [FLJ.53]

HOWARD, or ROCHE, MARY, widow of Richard Roche in Dublin, a will 1769, refers to her son Thomas, her friend James Goddard in Dublin, her nephew Alfred Goddard; wits. Edward in Dublin, Richard Moore, Valentine Ramsay in Dublin, Patrick Fitzgerald in Dublin. [DRD]

HOWE, MICHAEL, born 1781 in Dublin, a stonecutter in Charleston, South Carolina, naturalised there in 1813. [NARA.M1183]

HOWELL, THOMAS, was admitted as a Freeman of Dublin in 1691, [DLA]; a joiner in Dublin, a will, 1709. [DRD]

HOWISON, JOHN, in Dublin, will, 1746, brothers Thomas Howison, George Howison, Richard Howison, sisters, Hannah Howison, Elizabeth Howison, uncle Charles Howison, trustees – Henry Mitchell and Frederick Falkiner in Dublin; wits. Thomas Hall, Richard Brown Bamber, Hugh Ker a merchant, Elizabeth Howison, and George Donavan, in Dublin. [DRD]

HOYLE, JOSUA, Fellow of Trinity College, Dublin, 1618. [CSPIre]

HUCKERBY, JOHN, a slater, was admitted as a Freeman of Dublin in 1651, [DLA]; a helier and a brother of the Corporation of Carpenters in Dublin, 1656. [DCA.G2/1]

HUDSON, HENRY, a carpenter of Francis Street, Dublin, married Miss Benson, of Rainsford Street, Dublin, in 1766. [FDJ.4069]

HUGHES, FRANCIS ANNESLY, in Dublin, will, 1774, refers to his wife Mary Seayrs, his brother Thomas Hughes, his sister Deborah Hughes, his nephew Francis Annesly Hughes son of his brother John Hughes, his brother Paul Hughes, Attiwell Wood a counsellor at law, his nephew Paul Barker; wits. James Taylor a barrister at law, Andrew Hamilton a gentleman in Dublin, Joshua Hamilton a NP in Dublin, and William Costello a gentleman. [DRD]

HUGHES, GEORGE, a carpenter, was admitted as a Freeman of Dublin in 1655, [DLA]; a carpenter and a brother of the Corporation of Carpenters in Dublin, 1656. [DCA.G2/1]

HUGHES, ROBERT, former Customs Collector of Dublin, 1659. [CSPIre]; a gentleman in Swan Alley, Dublin, in 1659. [C]

HUGHES, THOMAS, in Dublin, a bond, 1680. [PRONI.D429.1]

HUMPHRYES, JOHN, a carpenter and a brother of the Corporation of Carpenters in Dublin, 1656. [DCA.G2/1]

HUMPHREYS, JOHN, in Dublin, will, 1775, refers to his nephew Richard Humphreys a clerk in County Kildare, his friend Robert Hamilton in Dublin second son of Alexander Hamilton, Thomas Humphreys a planter in Kingston, Jamaica, his nephew William Humphreys, kinsman John Butler godson Henry third son of said John Butler, Mary eldest daughter of said John Butler wife of Benjamin Yeates in Dublin, Margaret second daughter of said John Butler, Sarah youngest daughter of said John Butler, her cousin John Butler in Dublin and his nephew Richard Humphreys; wits. John Morris, Jon Chambers a timber merchant, and James Stafford all in Dublin. [DRD]

HUMPHREYS, WILLIAM, born 1681, an indentured servant aboard the Vine of Dublin landed in Middlesex County, Virginia, in 1693. [WI.193]

HUSBAND, JOHN, a joiner, was admitted as a Freeman of Dublin in 1655, [DLA]; a carpenter and a brother of the Corporation of Carpenters in Dublin, 1656. [DCA.G2/1]

HUSON, Mr, a linen-draper in Back Lane, Dublin, died in 1764. [FDJ.3841]

HUTCHESON, DANIEL, an Alderman of Dublin in 1669. [CSPIre]

INMAN, JOSEPH, a shearman, was admitted as a Freeman of Dublin in 1687, [DLA]; in Thomas Court, Dublin, 1701. [PRONI.D645.6]

INMAN, JOSEPH, was apprenticed to his father Joseph Inman a clothier in Thomas Court, Dublin, 1707. [PRONI.D645.11]

IVIE, GEORGE, in Dublin, a letter from New York, 1797. [SOD.Rebellion pp]

IRVING, WILLIAM, a laceman in Castle Street, Dublin, married Miss Anne Nesbitt, in 1766. [FDJ.4057]

JACKSON, HENRY, of St Patrick's in Dublin, probate 1691 PCC

JACKSON, HENRY, an ironmonger in Pill Lane, Dublin, married Miss Magrath of Usher's Island in 1766. [FDJ.4111]

JACKSON, I., a printer and bookseller, Meath Street, Dublin, 1751.

JACKSON, WILLIAM, a merchant from Boston, Lincolnshire, died in Dublin, probate 1698 PCC

JAMES, HENRY, a plasterer, was admitted as a Freeman of Dublin in 1654. [DLA]; a plasterer and a brother of the Corporation of Carpenters in Dublin, 1656. [DCA.G2/1]

THE PEOPLE OF DUBLIN, 1600-1799

JAMISON, JOHN, born 1784, a merchant in Dublin, emigrated aboard the Rover of New York , master George Bray, bound for New York in 1805. [BM.Addl.ms35762,103]

JANS, EDWARD, in Dublin, a bond, 1640. [PRONI.D430.145]

JANS, MARIA, widow of Francis Taylor in Dublin, a deed, 1650. [PRONI.D430.155]

JAQUEA, JUDITH, in Dublin, probate 1700 PCC

JAXON, WILLIAM, in Dublin, a deed, 1669. [PRONI.D509.20]

JEFFORD, Cornet, in St Bride's parish, Dublin, in 1659. [C]

JEFFERY, Mr, in Stevens Street, Dublin, 1659. [C]

JEFFREYS, JOHN, the Constable of Dublin Castle in 1673. [CSPDom.1673.527]

JENNINGS, RICHARD, a Fellow of Trinity College, Dublin, 1618. [CSPIre]

JEPHSON, JOHN, in Dublin, a deed, 1709. [PRONI.D665.19]

JERVIS, HUMPHREY, in Dublin, a lease, 1680. [PRONI.D366.1]

JOAKES, JOHN, a gentleman in Sheep Street, St Bride's parish, Dublin, 1659. [C]

JOHNSEY, THOMAS, in Dublin, a deposition, 1641. [PRONI.D1923.1.14.AR]

JOHNSON, ELIZABETH, in Dublin, and David Dempster in County Down, a marriage licence, Dublin, 1758. [PRONI.T1075.37]

JOHNSON, HENRY, born 1601, a merchant in Dublin, a witness before the High Court of the Admiralty of England in 1642, [TNA.HCA13.58.159]

JOHNSON, RANDEL, born 1691, died on the Coal Quay, Dublin, in 1766. [FDJ.4075]

JOHNSON, ROBERT, in Dublin, a letter, 1694. [PRONI.D778.16]

JOHNSTON, ARTHUR, in Dublin, a letter, 1765. [PRONI.D354.1024]

JOHNSTON, CATHERINE, in Henry Street, Dublin, married Samuel Yeates of Moone, County Kildare, in 1764. [FDJ.3840]

JOHNSTON, DAVID, master of the Betty and Sally of Dublin trading with Barbados in 1753. [PRONI.D354.537]

JOHNSTON, GILBERT, a carpenter, son of Gilbert Johnston a carpenter in Clarendon Street, Dublin, was admitted as a Freeman of Dublin in 1751. [DLA]

JOHNSTON, JOHN, a Quaker patternmaker, was admitted as a Freeman of Dublin in 1695. [DLA]

JOHNSTON, NATHANIEL, a cutler, spouse of Susanna Young, was admitted as a Freeman of Dublin in 1689. [DLA]

JOHNSTON, WILLIAM, of Mary's Lane, Dublin, married the widow Dean in Belfast, in 1764. [FDJ.3816]

JOHNSTON, Mrs, wife of Captain Johnston in Stephen's Green, Dublin, died in 1764. [FDJ.3842]

JONES, HENRY, a gentleman in Trinity Lane, College Green, Dublin, in 1659. [C]; in Dublin, a deed, 1674. [PRONI.T1878.14]

JONES. JOHN, a joiner and a brother of the Corporation of Carpenters in Dublin, 1656. [DCA.G2/1]; a joiner, was admitted as a Freeman of Dublin in 1656, [DLA];

JONES, JOHN, a tailor, was admitted as a Freeman of Dublin in 1734, [DLA]; a clothier on Pimlico, Dublin, died in 1766. [FDJ.4114]

JONES, MAURICE, a carpenter, was admitted as a Freeman of Dublin in 1636, [DLA]; a carpenter and a brother of the Corporation of Carpenters in Dublin, 1656. [DCA.G2/1]

JONES, RACHEL, in Dublin, an assignment of rights, 1708. [PRONI.D556.73]

JONES, RICHARD, a coachman in George's Lane, Dublin, a will, 1776, refers to his wife Frances, his children John, Francis, Robert and Sophia, his son in law Nicholas Grumly; wits. Reverend John Lyon curate of St Bridget's in Dublin, Thomas Tudor an attorney in Dublin, John Greanger a coach-maker in Dublin, Thomas Ferrall a coach-maker in Dublin, Thomas Darcy a clerk in Dublin. [DRD]

JONES, ROBERT, Fellow of Trinity College, Dublin, 1618. [CSPIre]

JONES, SAMUEL, a lodger in Damask Street, St Andrews parish, Dublin, in 1659. [C]

JONES, WILLIAM, a gentleman in Trinity Lane, College Green, Dublin, in 1659. [C]

JONES, Captain WILLIAM, a gentleman in Trinity Lane, College Green, Dublin, in 1659. [C]

JONES, Major WILLIAM, in Dublin, a letter, 1721. [PRONI.D10311]

JONES, ..., of Mountrath Street, Dublin, married Miss Price of Marlborough Street, Dublin, in 1766. [FDJ.4067]

JONQUIRE, Mr, messenger to the Incorporated Society and clerk to the French Society, died in George's Lane, Dublin, in 1764. [FDJ.3841]

KADE, GEORGE, a cutler and a member of the Guild of St Luke the Evangelist in Dublin in 1669. [CSPIre]; a cutler, was admitted as a Freeman of Dublin in 1654. [DLA]

THE PEOPLE OF DUBLIN, 1600-1799

KATHVENS, MURRAY, son of Samuel Kathvens, a merchant, was admitted as a Freeman of Dublin in 1753. [DLA]

KAVANAGH, PATRICK, a butcher in Patrick Street, Dublin, died in 1764. [FDJ.3845]

KEARNEY, JAMES, an attorney in 13 Mary Street, Dublin, a letter, 1800. [PRONI.D607A.590A]

KEARNEY, THOMAS, son of Michael Kearney, a barber, was admitted as a Freeman of Dublin in 1756. [DLA]

KEARNEY, Mrs, wife of Walter Kearney, died in Golden Lane, Dublin, in 1766. [FDJ.4130]

KEARSLEY, JOHN, a shoemaker, was admitted as a Freeman of Dublin in 1755. [DLA]

KEATING, DANIEL, a grocer in Dublin, a will, 1776, refers to his wife Elizabeth, and daughter Catherine; wits. John Quatermain a gentleman in Dublin, John Wilson a silk weaver in Dublin, and Martin Keating. [DRD]

KEATING, MICHAEL, in Dublin, a bond, 1770. [PRONI.D207.19.130]

KEATING, NICHOLAS, in Dublin, a will, 1752, wits Alexander Thompson a plumber, Thomas Gordon, William Devall NP, all of Dublin. [DRD]

KEATON, THOMAS, from Dublin, an indentured servant in Philadelphia, 1745. [EP.55]

KELLETT, RICHARD, a butcher, was admitted as a Freeman of Dublin in 1756. [DLA]

KELLY, ARTHUR, a weaver, son of John Kelly, was admitted as a Freeman of Dublin in 1735. [DLA]

KELLY, Major BRIEN, a Roman Catholic officer in Dublin in 1693. [CSPIre]

KELLY, CHRISTOPHER, a mariner from Dublin, was naturalised in Charleston, South Carolina, in 1804. [NARA.M1183]

KELLY, D., in Dublin, a letter, 1795. [NRAS.332.C3.2150]

KELLY, Captain EDMUND, a Roman Catholic officer in Dublin in 1693. [CSPIre]

KELLY, HENRY, a merchant in Dublin, 1602. [SPI.1602.400]

KELLY, JAMES, in Skinner Row, parish of St Nicholas within the Walls, Dublin, in 1659. [C]

KELLY, JAMES, a smith, was admitted as a Freeman of Dublin in 1753. [DLA]

KELLY, JOHN, a merchant was admitted as a Freeman of Dublin in 1756. [DLA]

KELLY, JOHN, of Bridge Street, Dublin, married Miss Swettenham of Nicholas Street, Dublin, in 1770. [FLJ.52]

KELLY, JOSEPH, a Quaker merchant, was admitted as a Freeman of Dublin in 1725.[DLA]

KELLY, LAUNCELOT, a gilder and glass-seller, died in Dame Street, Dublin, in 1764. [FDJ.3803]

KELLY, ROSE, daughter of Alderman Nicholas Kelly, was admitted as a Freeman of Dublin in 1629. [DLA]

KELLY, WILLIAM, a barber, former apprentice to Charles Kelly, was admitted as a Freeman of Dublin in 1704. [DLA]

KELLY, Mrs, wife of Mr Kelly in Patrick Street, Dublin, died in 1764. [FDJ.3927]

KENDALL, EDWARD, in Dublin, 1637. [NRS.GD406.1.381]

KENDALL, THOMAS, a shop-keeper to the late Mr Hyde and Mr Faulkner, died on College Green, Dublin, in 1766. [FDJ.4055]

KENNEDY, ANDREW, married Miss Richey of Duke Street, Dublin, in 1770. [FLJ.53]

KENNEDY, HUGH, jr., son of Hugh Kennedy, a shoemaker, was admitted as a Freeman of Dublin in 1753. [DLA]

KENNEDY, JAMES P., born 1794 in Dublin, an attorney in Charleston, South Carolina, naturalised 1821.[NARA.M1183]

KENNEDY, RICHARD, late grocer on Templebar, died in Grange Lane, Dublin, in 1766. [DRD]

KENNEDY, ROBERT, in Skinner Row, parish of St Nicholas within the Walls, Dublin, in 1659. [C]

KENNEDY, WALTER, a weaver, was admitted as a Freeman of Dublin in 1754. [DLA]

KENNY, HENRY, in Dublin, 1626/1628. [CPRIre]

KENNY, RICHARD, in Skinner Row, parish of St Nicholas within the Walls, Dublin, in 1659. [C]

KENT, JAMES, a paper stainer, was admitted as a Freeman of Dublin in 1756. [DLA]

KEOGH, JAMES, a brewer, James Street, Dublin, will, 1746, wife Jane Keogh, wits Patrick Fitzgerald victualler, Owen Mitchell clerk, Thomas Barnes ribbon weaver, William Hall clerk to James Saunders gentleman, all of Dublin. [DRD]

KERBY, LAWRENCE, a chairman in Dublin, will, 1773, refers to his wife Hannah Kerby, and children Margaret Kerby and Mary Kerby; wits. Andrew Kerby a gentleman in Dublin, Richard Taggart a cordwainer in Dublin, and Richard Henry Molley. [DRD]

KERRON, JOHN, a member of the Guild of Brewers in Dublin in 1669. [CSPIre]

KERSEY, JOHN, born 1603, a merchant in Dublin, a witness before the High Court of the Admiralty of England in 1639, [TNA.HCA13.54.396]

KETHRENS, GEORGE, jr., in Dublin, a petition, 1750. [PRONI.D207.23.26]

KEYLE, SAMUEL, a merchant, was admitted as a Freeman of Dublin in 1753. [DLA]

KICKHAM, THOMAS, in Skinner Row, parish of St Nicholas within the Walls, Dublin, in 1659. [C]; cf Thomas Kirkham, a barber surgeon, was admitted as a Freeman of Dublin in 1652. [DLA]

KIERNAN, EDWARD, of the Common Pleas Office in Dublin, died in Winetavern Street, Dublin, in 1766. [FDJ.4111]

KIERNAN, JAMES, a gentleman in Dublin, husband of Elizabeth ...., a will, 1709. [DRD]

KILBURNE, Mrs, wife of Mr Kilburne a book-binder, died in George's Lane, Dublin, in 1764. [FDJ'3827]

KILBY, WILLIAM, a tallow-chandler in Bride Street, Dublin, was admitted as a Freeman of Dublin in 1754. [DLA]; died in 1766. [FDJ.4046]

KILLIN, JAMES, at Trinity College, Dublin, a letter, 1756. [PRONI.D2707.A1.1.81A]

KIMBERLEY, EDWARD, a mason, was admitted as a Freeman of Dublin in 1756. [DLA]

KINCH, ALEXANDER, a shipwright, was admitted as a Freeman of Dublin in 1755. [DLA]

KING, ELIZABETH, daughter of Abraham King in Dublin, an indentured servant, bound for Virginia in 1698. [LRO]

KING, GEORGE, in Sheep Street, St Bride's parish, Dublin, 1659. [C]

KING, JAMES, in Dublin, a letter, 1784. [PRONI.D207.6.45]

KING, JOHN, a member of the Guild of Brewers in Dublin in 1669. [CSPIre]

KING, MACARELL, son of Robert King an alderman, was admitted as a Freeman of Dublin in 1753. [DLA]

KING, RALPH, in Skinner Row, parish of St Nicholas within the Walls, Dublin, in 1659. [C]

KING, ROBERT, Chamberlain to the Linen Hall of Dublin, a letter, 1780. [PRONI.D207.28.665]

KING, ROBERT, an attorney in Dublin, a letter, 1694; a deed, 1708. [PRONI.Dd683.238; D778.38]

KING, THOMAS, formerly an apprentice to Robert King, a tinplate worker, was admitted as a Freeman of Dublin in 1754. [DLA]

KING, THOMAS, son of George King, a hosier ?, was admitted as a Freeman of Dublin in 1756. [DLA]

KING, WILLIAM, Archbishop of Dublin, correspondence, 1704-1705. [TCD.mss1998-2008]

KING, Mrs, widow of Rev. Dr King, died in Kevan Street, Dublin, in 1764. [FDJ.3840]

KING, Mrs, a widow, died in Werburgh Street, Dublin, in 1764. [FDJ.3924]

KIRBY, WILLIAM, former apprentice to Antony Kirby, a founder, was admitted as a Freeman of Dublin in 1753. [DLA]

KIRK, PATRICK, from Dublin, an indentured servant in Philadelphia, 1745. [EP.55]

KITHINYMAN, JOHN, in Damask Street, St Andrews parish, Dublin, in 1659. [C]

KNIGHT, NICHOLAS, in Skinner Row, parish of St Nicholas within the Walls, Dublin, in 1659. [C]

KNIGHT, WILLIAM, in Dublin, probate 1674 PCC

KNOTT, ISAAC, a cooper, was admitted as a Freeman of Dublin in 1665. [DLA]; a cooper and member of the Fraternity of St Patrick's near Dublin in 1666. [CSPIre]

KNOTT, SAMUEL, a butcher, was admitted as a Freeman of Dublin in 1755. [DLA]

KNOTT, WALTER, a chandler, was admitted as a Freeman of Dublin in 1756. [DLA]

KNOX, GEORGE, a merchant, was admitted as a Freeman of Dublin in 1748. [DLA]; a merchant in Dublin, died in Londonderry in 1770. [FLJ.53]

KNOX, GEORGE, in Dublin, a letter, 1791. [PRONI.T2541.1B.1.2.23]

KNOX, SYMON, master of the Thomas and Ralph of Dublin was captured by Parliamentary forces when bound from Dublin to Liverpool in 1644. [TNA.IICA13.59.518/542].

KNOX, THOMAS, in Dublin, a letter, 1791. [PRONI.T2541.1B.1.2.39]

LA BASTIDE, ANTOINE MARTIN, a Huguenot soldier in the service of King William, died 1729 in Dublin, buried in St Patrick's. [HSP.XLI]

LACGER, JEAN JACQUES, born 1661, a Huguenot solder in the service of King William, died in Dublin 1761. [HSP.XLI.45]

LA FONT, ARMAND, a Huguenot soldier in the service of King William, died in Dublin in 1722. [HSP.XLI.46]

LAMBE, ANNE, niece of the late Councillor Lambe, died in James's Street, Dublin, in 1764. [FDJ.3927]

LA MAUGERE, MICHEL, a Huguenot soldier in the service of King William, died in Dublin in 1739. [HSP/XLI.51]

LA MOTTE, ANDRE, born 1637, a Huguenot soldier in the service of King William, died 1703 in Dublin. [HSP.XLI.54]

LANE, RICHARD, a joiner and a brother of the Corporation of Carpenters in Dublin, 1656. [DCA.G2/1]; a joiner, was admitted as a Freeman of Dublin in 1656. [DLA]

LANGLEY, JOHN, a merchant, son of James Langley, was admitted as a Freeman of Dublin in 1735. [DLA]

LANGLEY, JOHN, a surgeon, died on College Green, Dublin, in 1766. [FDJ.4101]

LANGON, FRANCOIS, a Huguenot soldier in the service of King William, died in Dublin in 1713. [HSP.XLI.47]

LANGTON, ABRAHAM, a citizen of Dublin who was imprisoned in 1663. [CSPIre]

LA RAMIERE, CLAUDE, born 1627, from Guienne, France, a Huguenot soldier in the service of King William, died in Dublin in 1693. [HSP.XLI.60]

LARGE, JOHN, a merchant in Dublin, 1602. [SPI.1602.400]

LARNEY, Mrs, wife of Mr Larney a shoemaker, died in Poolbeg Street, Dublin in 1764. [FDJ.3828]

LA SALLE, ANTHONY, a grocer in Portarlington, later in Dublin, will, 1746, son Isaac La Salle a grocer in Dublin, daughters Easter Horrell in Portarlington, and Gabriel Duff; wits Christopher Pazey, Charles Walker a grocer, John Ward a baker, John Kathrens NP, and his clerk Henry Steevens Reily, all in Dublin. [DRD]

LATROBE, Mrs, died in Fleet Street, Dublin, in 1764. [FDJ.3828]

LA TOUCHE, PETER, married Miss Vicars, in Dublin in 1766. [FDJ.4140]

LATROBE, Mr, died in Fleet Street, Dublin, in 1764. [FDJ.3828]

LAW, SAMUEL, a cutler, was admitted as a Freeman of Dublin in 1761. [DLA]

LAW, SAMUEL, a book-seller in Mountrath Street, Dublin, married Mrs Richon, a widow from County Wicklow in 1766. [FDJ.4039]

LAWLER, MATTHEW, died on George's Quay, Dublin, in 1764. [FDJ.3823]

LAWLESS, JAMES, a cooper and member of the Fraternity of St Patrick's near Dublin in 1666. [CSPIre]

LAWLIS, WILLIAM, a carpenter and a brother of the Corporation of Carpenters in Dublin, 1656. [DCA.G2/1]; a carpenter, was admitted as a Freeman of Dublin in 1638. [DLA]

LAWRENCE, PETER, master of the St John of Dublin trading with New England in 1680. [SPAWI.1680.1625]

LAWRENCE, RICHARD, a tallow chandler, was admitted as a Freeman of Dublin in 1669. [DLA]

LAWRENCE, RICHARD, a merchant, was admitted as a Freeman of Dublin in 1674. [DLA]

LAWRENCE, RICHARD, a gentleman in Dublin, probate 1691 PCC

LAYFIELD, LEWIS, a gentleman, Martins Lane, Dublin, will, 1750, wife Sarah Layfield, wits. Ann Lawrence his daughter, William Holt, and William Carmichael, all in Dublin. [DRD]

LEADER, JOHN, in Dublin, a lease, 1768. [PRONI.D1255.4.13A]

LEATHAM, HUGH, a grocer in Abbey Street, Dublin, died in 1764. [FDJ.3842]

LECORA, Lieutenant, in St Bride's parish, Dublin, in 1659. [C]

LEDWICH, RICHARD, a cooper and member of the Fraternity of St Patrick's near Dublin in 1666. [CSPIre]; a cooper, was admitted as a Freeman of Dublin in 1675. [DLA]

LEE, Mrs JANE, wife of Richard Lee, died in White Friar Street, Dublin, in 1763. [FDJ.3725]

LEE, JOHN, an inn-keeper in Dublin, 1727. [CPRIre]

LEE, JOHN, of the GPO in Dublin, died 1766. [FDJ.4137]

LEE, THOMAS, a cook in Dublin, took the Oath of Allegiance and Supremacy to King Charles II in 1666.

LEES, EDWARD S., in Dublin, was admitted as a burgess and guilds-brother of Ayr in 1801. [ABR]

LEES, JOHN, in Dublin, was admitted as a burgess and guilds-brother of Ayr in 1801. [ABR]

LE FERON, PAUL, from Metz, France, a Huguenot soldier in the service of King William, died 1713 in Dublin. [HSP.XLI.38]

LEGGAT, WILLIAM, master of the Hopewell of Dublin 1699. [TNA.CO5.1441]

LELAND, Reverend JOHN, DD, born 1691, died in Eustace Street, Dublin, in 1766. [FDJ.4041]

LELAND, Mrs, a widow, died in Ann Street near the Linen Hall, Dublin, in 1764. [FDJ.3810]

LEMOND, CHARLES, a gentleman in St Geoge's Lane, parish of St Andrew, Dublin, in 1659. [C]

LENAGHAN, JOHN, a carver and gilder, died in Kevan Street, Dublin, in 1764. [FDJ.3927]

LENNON, Mrs, in Queen Street, Dublin, died 1764. [FDJ.3841]

LEONARD, Mrs, wife of Mr Leonard a publican, died in Christchurch Lane, Dublin, in 1764. [FDJ.3814]

LEPLAND, Lieutenant, a Roman Catholic officer in Dublin in 1693. [CSPIre]

LESCURE, JOHN, a sugar baker in George's Lane, Dublin, died in 1766. [FDJ.4081]

LEVALLIN, Captain MILTHER, a Roman Catholic officer in Dublin in 1693. [CSPIre]

LEVENTHORPE, RALPH, in Dublin, a lease, 1629. [PRONI.D430.126]

LEVER, RALPH, a mariner in Dublin, died aboard HMS Southampton, probate, 1700 PCC

LEWIS, THOMAS, a boxmaker and a brother of the Corporation of Carpenters in Dublin, 1656. [DCA.G2/1]; a boxmaster, was admitted as a Freeman of Dublin in 1638. [DLA]

LEWIS, Mrs, wife of Benjamin Lewis a grocer, died in Nicholas Gate, Dublin, in 1764. [FDJ.3818]

LIGER, SALOMAN, born 1646 in Loudun, Vienne, France, a Huguenot soldier in the service of King William, died in Dublin 1722 and buried in St Patrick's. [HSP.XLI.48]

LILL, GODREY, in Dublin, a letter, 1754. [PRONI.T2863.1.70]

LINCOLN, NICHOLAS, alderman and merchant in Dublin, a petition, 1710. [TNA.SP34.30.23A]

LINDSEY, ANN, born 1769, from Dublin, died on Madeira on 26 May 1828. [ARM]

LINDSAY, HENRY, a woollen draper, died in High Street, Dublin, in 1764. [FDJ.3823]

LINDSEY, Mr, in Dame Street, Dublin, married Miss Elizabeth Tweedy, in 1766. [FDJ.4058]

LINEGAR, JOHN, a slater, was admitted as a Freeman of Dublin in 1649. [DLA]; a helier and a brother of the Corporation of Carpenters in Dublin, 1656. [DCA.G2/1]

LINGARD, RICHARD, a senior fellow of Trinity College, Dublin, in 1661. [CSPIre]

LINGUM, ROBERT, a mariner in Dublin, died at sea, probate 1673 PCC

LISTER, GEORGE, master of the Mary of Dublin trading with France in 1692. [CSPDom.1692.148][CTB.IX.1636]

LITTLE, FRANCIS, a gentleman in Trinity Lane, College Green, Dublin, in 1659. [C]

LITTLE, HENRY, in Dublin, 1627. [CPRIre]

LITTLE, JOHN, late of Dublin, and his sisters Rica and Katherine, 1627. [CPRIre]

LITTLEHALES, Sir E. B., in Dublin Castle, a letter, 1804. [PRONI.D562.9972]

LLOYD, PATRICK, born 1625, from Dublin, a seaman aboard the Michael of Wyne, a witness before the High Court of the Admiralty of England in 1646. [TNA.HCA13.60.525.159]

LOANES, JAMES, in Dublin, a lease of premises in the High Street of Dublin, 1680. [PRONI.D514.4]

LOCK, Quartermaster RICHARD, a Roman Catholic officer in Dublin in 1693. [CSPIre]

LOFTUS, Dr DUDLEY, in Dublin, 1673. [CSPDom.1673.527]

LOFTUS, NICHOLAS, in Dublin, a bond, 1637. [PRONI.D430.142]

LOMBARD, DOMINICK, a gentleman in Dublin, a deed, 1674. [PRONI.D61.1]

LONCHANT, ..., a Huguenot soldier in the service of King William, died in Dublin 1703. [HSP.XLI.49]

LONGFORD, Sir HERCULES, in Dublin, a deed, 1680. [PRONI.D723]

LORD, ANDREW, merchant in Wine Tavern Street, Dublin, 1659. [C]

LORD, Mrs, wife of Francis Lord a gunsmith in Dame Street, Dublin, died in 1764. [FDJ.3842]

LOTCHARD, PETER, a cooper, was admitted as a Freeman of Dublin in 1653. [DLA]; Warden of the Corporation of Carpenters in Dublin in 1656. [DCA.G2/1]

LOVAT, JOHN, a merchant in Dublin, a petition, 1689. [CTB.IX.297]

LOWTHER, JOHN, in Dublin, probate 1697 PCC

LOWTHER, JOHN, in Dublin, a deed, 1733. [PRONI.D671D.11.1.2]

LOWTHER, LUKE, a cooper and a brother of the Corporation of Carpenters in Dublin, 1656. [DCA.G2/1];a cooper and member of the Fraternity of St Patrick's near Dublin in 1666; a member of the Guild of Brewers in Dublin in 1669. [CSPIre]

LLOYD, Quartermaster, a gentleman in Trinity Lane, College Green, Dublin, in 1659. [C]

LUDLOW, GEORGE, a plasterer and a brother of the Corporation of Carpenters in Dublin, 1656. [DCA.G2/1]

LUFFINGHAM, BENJAMIN, died in Fishshamble Street, Dublin, in 1766. [FDJ.4073]

LUNEL, PETER, born 1652 in Le Havre, France, a Huguenot soldier in the service of King William, died in Dublin in 1720. [HSP.XLI.49]

LUNEMAN, SIMON, in Dublin, 1748, mother Susanna wife of Michael Tramasse, a merchant, wits Mary Welsh and Henry Hawkins all in Dublin. [DRD]

LUTIS, JAMES, master of the Francis and Elizabeth of Dublin trading with Barbados in 1703. [TNA.CO33.13]

LYNCH, Lieutenant PATRICK, a Roman Catholic officer in Dublin in 1693. [CSPIre]

LYNCH, TERENCE, died in Winetavern Street, Dublin, in 1764. [FDJ.3927]

LYNCH, ..., a carpenter, married Biddy French, a milliner in Britain Street, Dublin, in 1766. [FDJ.4108]

LYNDON, Mrs ANN, widow of John Lyndon of Frederick Street, died in Ann Street, Dublin, in 1766. [FDJ.4078]

LYNDON, JOHN, in Dublin, a deed, 1674. [PRONI.T1878.1]

LYNES, RICHARD, a helier and a brother of the Corporation of Carpenters in Dublin, 1656. [DCA.G2/1]; a slater, was admitted as a Freeman of Dublin in 1655. [DLA]

LYNFORD, ..., died in Britain Street, Dublin, in 1766. [FDJ.4114]

LYONS, ELEANOR, of Lower Castle Yard, Dublin, married Thomas Ivory in 1764. [FDJ.3829]

MACADAM, JOHN, a cooper and a brother of the Corporation of Carpenters in Dublin, 1656. [DCA.G2/1]

MCALLISTER, JOHN, a merchant in Dublin, 1776. [NLI]

MCALESTAR, ROBERT, of the General Post Office, Dublin, married Ann Mackerness of Meeting-house Yard, Dublin, in 1766. [FDJ.4103]

MCAULAY, ALEXANDER, a counsellor at law, the Rowen, Nicholson Street, Dublin, a letter, 1732; a deed, 1736. [PRONI.D162.26; T810.1.4]

MCCARTHY, RICHARD, master of the Diana of Dublin trading with Philadelphia in 1740. [PhilaGaz]

MACARTNEY, A. C., in Dublin, a letter, 1800. [PRONI.D572.12.112]

MCCAUSLAND, W., in Dublin, a letter, 1700s. [PRONI.D669.211]

MCCLINTOCK, Mrs, wife of Alexander McClintock, died in Dominick Street, Dublin, in 1764. [FDJ.3810]

MCCLURE, HAMILTON, in Dublin, a bond, 1775. [PRONI.D300.3.3.1]

MCCORMICK, JEREMIAH, of the Bachelor's Walk, Dublin, married Barbara Connolly of Templebar, Dublin, in 1770. [FLJ.53]

MCCOY, ALEXANDER, a wig-maker, was admitted as a Freeman of Dublin in 1701. [DLA]

MCCOY, MICHAEL, a coach-maker, was admitted as a Freeman of Dublin in 1771. [DLA]

MCCULLAGH, JOHN, born 1799, from Dublin, died on Madeira in 1825. [ARM]

MCDONNEL, CHARLES, a coach-maker in Dublin, married Miss Dalton, in 1766. [FDJ.4072]

MCDONNELL, JOHN, a grocer in William Street, Dublin, married Miss Fitzgerald of Peter Street, Dublin, in 1764. [FDJ.3830]

MACDONNELL, MARY, in Dublin, and Rowley Heyland in Belfast, a marriage settlement, 1780. [PRONI.D300.1.6.6]

MCDONNELL, THOMAS, an apothecary, was admitted as a Freeman of Dublin in 1763. [DLA]

MCDONNELL, THOMAS, a merchant, formerly an apprentice of Alexander McDonnell, was admitted as a Freeman of Dublin in 1767. [DLA]

MCGEE, THOMAS, a silk weaver in Pill Lane, Dublin, married Miss McAvoy of said place, in 1770. [FLJ.50]

MAGILL, JOHN, a peruke maker in Dublin, a will, 1772, refers to his wife Elizabeth, their children Rachell, William, and John, William Ker and William Maddock both gentlemen in Dublin, [DRD]

MCGILL, THOMAS, in Dublin, was admitted as a burgess and guilds-brother of Ayr in 1802. [ABR]

MCGRATH, Reverend JAMES, born 1766, educated at Trinity College, Dublin, later Rector of Toronto, died 1851 in Erindale, Upper Canada. [GM.ns36.327]

MCGUIRE, CONSTANTINE, from Dublin, an indentured servant in Philadelphia, Pennsylvania, 1745. [EP.55]

MAGUIRE, Colonel HUGH, in Jervais Street, Dublin, died in 1766. [FDJ.4067]

MCKEVERS, ALEXANDER, a publican in Great Britain Street, Dublin, died in 1766. [FDJ.4115]

MCLAUGHLIN, Mrs, wife of Mr McLaughlin a grocer in Poolbeg Street, Dublin, died in 1764. [FDJ.3928]

MACLEAN, ALLAN, of Dublin Customs House, a letter, 1802. [PRONI.D562.5876]

MCMAHON, Reverend DOMINICK, born 1696, late of Drogheda, died in Brick Lane, Dublin, in 1766. [FDJ.4120]

MCMANUS, WILLIAM, a japanner, was admitted as a Freeman of Dublin in 1757. [DLA]

MCPHERSON, ANNA, relict of Robert Cook in Dublin, testament, 1725 Commissariat of Edinburgh. [NRS]

MCRAE, JAMES, master of the Bonadventure of Dublin trading with Cadiz, Spain, in 1705, [CalSPDom.SP44.390.320]; master of the Union Galley of Dublin trading with Madeira and Antigua in 1708. [TNA.CO157.1]

MCWILLIE, JOHN, in Dublin, a lease, 1777. [PRONI.D462.19]

MADDEN, EDWARD, married Charlotte, daughter of Abraham Creighton , in Dublin in 1766. [FDJ.4077]

MAGUIRE, FELIX, a salesmaster, died in Bow Street, Dublin, in 1764. [FDJ.3809]

MAILLET, PIERRE, born in Montelimar, France, a Huguenot soldier in the service of King William, died 1740 in Dublin. [HSP.XLI.49]

MALONE, Mrs, wife of William Malone, died on Usher's Quay in Dublin in 1766. [FDJ.4060]

MANDEVIL, Captain PATRICK, a Roman Catholic officer in Dublin in 1693. [CSPDom.1693.16]

MANNEY, RALPH, a gentleman in St George's Lane, parish of St Andrew, Dublin, in 1659. [C]

MANNING, MARY, daughter of Mr Manning a timber merchant, died in Patrick Street, Dublin, in 1764. [FDJ.3930]

MANSFIELD, FRANCIS, in Dublin, a letter, 1792. [PRONI.T2541.1B.3.3.53]

MANT, ..., of Harold's Cross, Dublin, married Elinor Collins of Booter Lane, Dublin, in 1770. [FLJ.51]

MANWARING, WILLIAM, a toyman in George's Lane, Dublin, will, 1769, refers to his wife Virtue, his children James, Catherine, Virue, Mary, and Sarah; wits. John Kiernan in Dublin, Edmond Dunn in Dublin, William Fitzgerald and his wife Henrietta in Dublin. [DRD]

MARGETSON, ANNE, a widow in Dublin, probate 1685 PCC

MARKHAM, ..., in St Bride's parish, Dublin, in 1659. [C]

MARLEY, MANUS, from Dublin, an indentured servant in Philadelphia, Pennsylvania, 1745. [EP.54]

MARROW, WILLIAM, a cooper, was admitted as a Freeman of Dublin in 1654. [DLA]; a cooper and a brother of the Corporation of Carpenters in Dublin, 1656. [DCA.G2/1]

MARSDEN, A., in Dublin Castle, a letter, 1804. [PRONI.D207.26.118]

MARSDEN and BENSON, in Dublin, a letter, 1775. [PRONI.D354.883]

MARSH, FRANCIS, Archbishop of Dublin, probate 1693 PCC

MARSH, MARY, a widow in Dublin, probate 1695 PCC

MARSH, SAMUEL, in Dublin, probate 1663/1671 PCC

MARSHALL, MATTHEW, a merchant in Dublin, testament, 1711 Commissariat of Edinburgh

MARTIN, Colonel GARRET, in Dublin, a Roman Catholic who was licenced to bear arms in 1705. [HMC.Ormond.ii.476]

MARTIN, SAMUEL, in Dublin, a letter, 1682. [PRONI.D1618.15.2.43]

MASON, JOHN, formerly of Trinity College, Dublin, died in Fishshambles Street, Dublin, in 1766. [FDJ.4126]

MASSAM, WILLIAM, a gentleman in Dublin, probate 1623 PCC

MATTHEWS, EDWARD, in Dublin, a will, 1758, refers to his wife Sarah and their children Daniel, Hill, Edward, Andrew, John, Elizabeth, Grace, Sarah, Jane, Ann, Charlotte, Leslie, and Mary; wits. Pierce Byrne a gentleman, Valentine Ramsay a merchant, William Owen a gentleman, and Thomas Gardiner, all in Dublin. [DRD]

MATTHEWES, JOHN, a gardener in Drumcondra Lane, Dublin, died in 1764. [FDJ.3805]

MATTHEWS, Captain FRANCIS, a Roman Catholic officer in Dublin in 1693. [CSPDom.1693.16]

MATHEW, JOHN, in Dublin, a letter, 1691. [PRONI.D429.36]

MATHEW, MORGAN, in Dublin, probate 1626 PCC

MATURIN, WILLIAM, of the General Post Office, married Miss Watson of Marlborough Street, Dublin, in 1770. [FLJ.50]

MAULE, THOMAS, in Dublin, 1640. [NRS.GD504.9.98]; a gentleman in St Geoge's Lane, parish of St Andrew, Dublin, in 1659. [C]

MAXWELL, GEORGE, in St Bride's parish, Dublin, in 1659. [C]

MAY, HENRY, in Dublin Castle, a letter, 14 December 1699. [TCD.750.652]

MAY, WALTER, a tailor in Christ Church Yard, Dublin, a will, 1682. [NAI.999.18]

MAY, WILLIAM, a merchant in Dublin, a will, 1687. [NAI.999.18]

MAZIERE, LINNY, eldest daughter of Mr Maziere a merchant in Fleet Street, Dublin, married Peter Gallant a merchant in Belfast in 1764. [FDJ.3791]

MEADE, ROBERT, a member of the Guild of Brewers in Dublin in 1669. [CSPIre]

MEADE, ..., son of Sir John Meade, was born in Merrion Street, Dublin, in 1766. [FDJ.4074]

MEAGHE, JOHN, an almsman in Dublin, a petition, 1601? [SPI.1601.647.

MEAKIN, ELIZABETH, born 1688, a spinster from Dublin, an indentured servant bound for America in 1704. [LRO]

MEE, GILES, a member of the Guild of Brewers in Dublin in 1669. [CSPIre]

MEE, JOHN, in Dublin, a deed, 1777, [PRONI.D366.96]

MELVILL, DAVID, a merchant in Dublin, was admitted as a burgess and guilds-brother of Ayr in 1767. [ABR]; a merchant, was admitted as a Freeman of Dublin in 1771. [DLA]

MEREDITH, ARTHUR, in Dublin, a lease, 1670. [PRONI.T2125.12.4]

MEREDITH, Sir CHARLES, in Dublin, probate 1700 PCC

MEREDITH, HENRY, in Dublin, a lease, 1770s. [PRONI.D234.6]

MEREDITY, ARTHUR, in Dublin, a deed, 1671. [PRONI.D526.1.1]

MEREDITY, DOROTHY, in Dublin, a deed, 1671. [PRONI.D526.1.1]

THE PEOPLE OF DUBLIN, 1600-1799

MERRICK, Cornet, a gentleman in Trinity Lane, College Green, Dublin, in 1659. [C]

MERVIN, Sir AUDLEY, in Dublin, a deed, 1665. [PRONI.D389.6]

MERVYN, WILLIAM, a butcher in St Patrick Street, Dublin, was denisized in Ireland in 1665. [IPR]

MESLER, Captain, died on George's Quay, Dublin, in 1766. [FDJ.4075]

MILLER, NATHANIEL, a butcher in Dublin, a lease, 1706. [PRONI.D236.1]

MILLS, JOHN, a carpenter and a brother of the Corporation of Carpenters in Dublin, 1656. [DCA.G2/1]

MILLS, MARGARET, wife of James Mills, late of Allen, County Kildare, died in Pudding Row, Dublin, in 1764. [FDJ.3829]

MILNER, JACOB, a book-seller in Essex Street, Dublin, in 1695. [NLI]

MITCHELL, Mrs, mother of ... Mitchell a book-seller in Skinner Row, Dublin, died in Dorset Street, Dublin, in 1766. [FDJ.4113]

MOLESWORTH, or JOHNSTON, LETITIA, wife of George Johnston in Dublin, refers to John Moland in Dublin, Richard Holmes in Dublin, her brothers Captain Robert Molesworth and Richard Molesworth, her sisters Juliana Herbert, Jane Clootwyk, Amelia Molesworth, Isabella Molesworth and Elizabeth Holmes, niece Letitia Herbert, cousin Lieutenant Richard Lambert, John Lambe a counsellor at law, Thomas Coghlan a merchant in Dublin son of the late John Coghlan and grandson of the late Dr Henry Maule the Bishop of Meath; wits. John Lambert and Laurence Pearson gentlemen in Dublin, Henry Maguire clerk to Thomas Coghlan, and Bryan Meheux. [DRD]

MOLOGHLIN, JAMES, in Thomas Court, Dublin, a deed, 1701. [PRONI.D645.6]

MONCK, THOMAS, an attorney in Dublin, 1771. [PRONI.D128.1]

MONES, CHARLES, in Dublin, an indenture, 1733. [PRONI.D207.19.51]

MONNEY, Mr, of Hog Hill, married Miss Sherlock of George's Lane, Dublin, in 1765. [FDJ.3935]

MONTGOMERY, Captain HUGH, in Dublin, a mortgage, 1670. [PRONI.T1878.10]

MONTGOMERY, WILLIAM, a merchant in Dublin, was admitted as a burgess and guilds-brother of Glasgow in 1717. [GBR]

MOONEY, JOHN, a cooper, was admitted as a Freeman of Dublin in 1653. [DLA]; a cooper and a brother of the Corporation of Carpenters in Dublin, 1656. [DCA.G2/1]

MOORE, Sir CHARLES in Dublin, will, 1754, refers to John the Earl of Egmont, Henry Prittie of Kilboy, uncle Robert Moore, sisters Catherina Putland and Ann Moore, William Percival second son of Dean Percival of Dublin, John Putland, and William Percival, both of Dublin; wits. Benjamin Johnston NP, and his clerks Anthony Ivers and Robert Jones, all in Dublin. [DRD]

MOORE, FRANCIS, a joiner, was admitted as a Freeman of Dublin in 1654. [DLA]; a joiner and a brother of the Corporation of Carpenters in Dublin, 1656. [DCA.G2/1]

MOORE, HENRY, in Dublin, a bond, 1769. [PRONI.D207.19.120]

MOORE, JANE, in Dublin, a deed of annuity, 1776. [PRONI.D359.2]

MOORE, JOHN, in Stevens Street, Dublin, 1659. [C]

MOORE, Captain JOHN, a Roman Catholic officer in Dublin in 1693. [CSPDom.1693.16]

MOORE, JOHN, son of John Moore, a merchant in Dublin, was admitted as a burgess and guilds-brother of Ayr in 1726. [ABR]

THE PEOPLE OF DUBLIN, 1600-1799

MOORE, JOHN, a glover in Dame Street, Dublin, died in 1766.
[FDJ.4069]

MOORE, MARGARET, a spinster in Dublin, a will, 1710. [CPRI]

MOORE, SUSANNAH, in Dublin, a letter, 1728. [PRONI.D562.532]

MOORE, SYMON, a carpenter, was admitted as a Freeman of Dublin in 1735. [DLA]; a carpenter and a brother of the Corporation of Carpenters in Dublin, 1656. [DCA.G2/1]

MOREN, GEORGE, from Dublin, a shipbuilder in Philadelphia, Pennsylvania, a Loyalist in 1776, later settled in Halifax, Nova Scotia, by 1786. [TNA.AO12.75.1]

MORGAN, SAMUEL, formerly officer to the Dublin Common Council, died in Dawson Street, Dublin, in 1766. [FDJ.4079]

MOROLY, JAMES, in St Bride's parish, Dublin, in 1659. [C]

MORPITT, JOHN, a tailor from London, died in Dublin, probate 1695 PCC

MORRIS, Captain HARVEY, a Roman Catholic officer in Dublin in 1693. [CSPDom.1693.16]

MORRIS, RICHARD, in Prussia Street, Dublin, a will, 1770, refers to his wife Ann; wits. Edmond McCan in Dublin, John Alexander in Dublin, and William Jones a shoemaker in Dublin. [DRD]

MORRIS, THOMAS, a former Customs Collector in Dublin in 1659. [CSPIre]

MOSS, JACOB, a cabinet maker in Mary Street, Dublin, will, 1785, refers to his wife Mary Ann Murphy, their children Catherine, Patrick, and Elizabeth, his mother Elizabeth Hogan, Precious Clark a merchant in

Dublin, Francis Bourke a victualler, John Bouchier a confectioner in College Street, Dublin, wits. William Flood a sailmaker in Dublin, Richard Supple a publican in Dublin, John Nugent a hairdresser in Dublin, and Patrick Little a gentleman in Dublin. [DRD]

MOTLEY, WALTER, a merchant in Dublin, 1673. [CSPDom.1673.527]; was admitted as a Freeman of Dublin in 1688. [DLA]

MOULD, Dr ROBERT, a gentleman in Trinity Lane, College Green, Dublin, in 1659. [C]

MOULSWORTH, ROBERT, a merchant in Dublin, to transport felons in Newgate gaol, Dublin, to Barbados or other English plantation in America in 1656, [IC.II.777]; 'died beyond the seas', probate 1657 PCC

MOYNES,......, a gentleman in Golden Lane, St Bride's parish, Dublin, 1659. [C]

MUCKLEBORNE, ABRAHAM, a gentleman in St Geoge's Lane, parish of St Andrew, Dublin, in 1659. [C]

MUIR, JOHN, a merchant in Dublin, was admitted as a burgess and guilds-brother of Glasgow in 1717. [GBR]

MULLAN, DANIEL, a peruke-maker in Dublin, and his apprentice John Bradley, an apprenticeship indenture, 1695. [Inchiquin ms1236]

MULLIGAN, ANN, in Dublin, a petition, 1766. [PRONI.D207.23.3]

MULLOCKE, JOHN, a cooper and a brother of the Corporation of Carpenters in Dublin, 1656. [DCA.G2/1]

MULOCK, MARY, wife of Thomas Mulock, died in Skinner Row, Dublin, in 1766. [FDJ.4116]

MURPHY, JAMES, a carpenter, was admitted as a Freeman of Dublin in 1654. [DLA]; a carpenter and a brother of the Corporation of Carpenters in Dublin, 1656. [DCA.G2/1]

MURPHY, JAMES, master of the Dove of Dublin trading between Cardigan and Dublin in 1705. [TNA.SP63.366.63]

MURPHY, JOHN, a shipbuilder in White's Lane, Dublin, married Mrs Adair of George's Quay, Dublin, in 1764. [FDJ.3833]

MURPHY, RICHARD, master of the Lamb of Dublin trading with Virginia in 1699-1700. [LRO][TNA.CO5.1311]; master of the Dove of Dublin trading with Catalonia, Spain, in 1705. [TNA.SP42.119.183]

MURPHY, Mrs, wife of Mr Murphy an attorney, died in Jervais Street, Dublin, in 1766. [FDJ.4122]

MURRAY, ALEXANDER, in Great Booter's Lane, Dublin, died in 1770. [FLJ.51]

MURRAY, ROBERT, a tailor in Dublin, was admitted as a Freeman of Belfast in 1730. [TBB]

MURTH, THOMAS, master of the Robert of Dublin trading with San Sebastien in Spain, 1705. [CalSPDom.SP44.393.95]

MUSCHAMP, WILLIAM, a former Customs Collector in Dublin in 1659. [CSPIre]

MUSSENDEN, WILLIAM, in Dublin, a lease, 1775. [PRONI.D491.31]

NANGLE, Colonel FRANCIS, a Roman Catholic officer in Dublin in 1693. [CSPDom.1693.16]

NASH, DAVID, a Roman Catholic prisoner in Dublin, to be released on condition that he moved to Connaught in 1657. [IC.ii.918]

NEALE, ARTHUR, was admitted as a Freeman of Dunlin in 1638, [DLA];a plasterer and a brother of the Corporation of Carpenters in Dublin, 1656. [DCA.G2/1]

NEALE, DENNIS, a cooper and a member of the Fraternity of St Patrick's near Dublin in 1666. [CalSPIre]; was admitted as a Freeman of Dublin in 1674. [DLA]

NEALE, THOMAS, porter of Dublin Castle, 1626. [CPRIre]

NEALE, Mrs, wife of William Neale master of the Great Music Hall of Dublin, died in Fishshamble Street, Dublin, in 1763. [FDJ.3725]

NEEDHAM, ANDREW, a merchant in Anglesea Street, Dublin, died in 1766. [FDJ.4096]

NEELD, JOHN, a carpenter and a brother of the Corporation of Carpenters in Dublin, 1656. [DCA.G2/1]

NEINEY, Mrs MARGARET, died in Great Britain Street, Dublin, in 1766. [FDJ.4045]

NEISFIELD, JOSHUA, a tanner, died in James's Street, Dublin, in 1764. [FDJ.3790]

NETTERVILL, Captain JAMES, a Roman Catholic officer in Dublin in 1693. [CSPDom.1693.16]; licensed to bear arms in 1705. [HMC.Ormond.II.476]

NETTERVILL, LUKE, brother of Lord Nettervill, a Roman Catholic in Dublin, licensed to bear arms in 1705. [HMC.Ormond.ii.476]

NEVIN, DAVID, a publican in Thomas Street, Dublin, died in 1764. [FDJ.3840]

NEWBERRY, NATHANIEL, a gentleman from Portsmouth, Hampshire, later in Dublin, probate 1681 PCC

NEWCOMEN, THOMAS, of Dublin, the Customer, Collector, and Receiver of the Customs of the city of Cork, 1626. [CPRIre]

NEWLAND, CATHERINE, relict of William Newland a coach-maker, died in Anglesea Street, Dublin, in 1764. [FDJ.3787]

NEWLAND, GEORGE, in Meath Street, Dublin, a deed, 1698. [PRONI.D645.5]

NEWMAN, Captain ROBERT, in Golden Lane, St Bride's parish, Dublin, 1659. [C]

NEWMAN, ROBERT, a gentleman in Golden Lane, St Bride's parish, Dublin, 1659. [C]

NEWPORT, MATTHEW, a weaver in Skinner's Alley on the Coomb, Dublin, died in 1770. [FLJ.51]

NICHOLLS, Captain JOHN, a gentleman in Lazy Hill, College Green, Dublin, in 1659. [C]

NICHOLSON, GILBERT, in Dublin, a will, 1709. [DRD]

NICHOLSON, Mr, a watchmaker, died in Crane Lane, Dublin, in 1766. [FDJ.4085]

NICHOLSON, ..., in Great Britain Street, Dublin, 1790. [PRONI.D207.19.161A]

NIMMO, WILLIAM, master of the Virgin Queen of Dublin trading with Charleston, South Carolina, in 1739. [TNA.CO5.510]

NIXON, DANIEL, was admitted as a Freeman of Dublin in 1652, [DLA]; a carpenter and a brother of the Corporation of Carpenters in Dublin, 1656. [DCA.G2/1]

NOLSOR, DAVID, master of the Thomas of Dublin trading with Bilbao in Spain, 1705. [TNA.SP.392.54]

NORTH, F., in Dublin, a letter, 1728. [PRONI.D562.370]

NORTH, JOHN, a stationer and a member of the Guild of St Luke the Evangelist in Dublin, 1669. [CalSPIre]

NORTON, BRETT, born 1692, late Captain of the 12th Regiment of Dragoons, died at his brother's house in Dorset Street, Dublin, in 1765. [FDJ.3935]

NORTON, HENRY, a merchant in Dublin, co-owner of the <u>Mary Ann of Liverpool</u> registered at the Customs House of Liverpool in 1742.

NOWLANE, DANIEL, in Dublin, a lease, 1601. [PRONI.D430.106]

NOWLAN, JOHN, a robber, was executed at Stephen's Green, Dublin, in 1765. [FDJ.3932]

NOWLAN, Mr, a vintner in Cook Street, Dublin, died in 1764. [FDJ.3842]

NOYSE, RICHARD, a gentleman in Dublin, probate 1697 PCC

NUGENT, JAMES, was admitted as a Freeman of Dublin in 1615, [DLA]; a merchant in Dublin, who was shipwrecked off Cornwall then robbed by the inhabitants in 1622. [CSPIre]

NUGENT, MICHAEL, a Roman Catholic in Dublin, licenced to bear arms in 1705. [HMC.Ormond.ii.476]

NUGENT, OLIVER, married Eleanora Irvine, in Frederick Street, Dublin, in 1766. [FDJ.4086]

NUGENT, Captain WALTER, a Roman Catholic officer in Dublin in 1693. [CSPDom.1693.16]

NUGENT, WILLIAM, a jeweller in Skinner Row, Dublin, married Miss Fisher of Queen Street, Dublin, in 1764. [FDJ.3781]

NY DUNGAN, HONOR, was pardoned in Dublin in 1608. [HMC.Hastings.iv.32]

OB, THOMAS, in Stevens Street, Dublin, 1659. [C]

O'DOLAN, TIRLAGH, was pardoned in Dublin in 1608. [HMC.Hastings.iv.32]

O'GALLAGHER, SIMON FELIX, born in Dublin 1762, was naturalised in South Carolina in 1802. [NARA.M1183]

O'HARA, KEAN, in Dublin, a letter, 1698. [PRONI.T2812.4.274]

O'KELLIE, JOHN NAMOY, a scholar at Trinity College, Dublin, in 1618. [CSPIre]

O'KENNEDY, PHILIP, was pardoned in Dublin in 1608. [HMC.Hastings.iv.32]

OLIVER, JOHN, a shoemaker, died in High Street, Dublin, in 1764. [FDJ.3803]

O'NEILL, BRIAN, in Dublin, a letter, 1671. [PRONI.T2812.2.1]

O'NEILL, JOHN, a butcher in Ormond Market, Dublin, died in 1766. [FDJ.4118]

O'NEILL, LAURENCE, an Irish Episcopal priest, ordained by William King the Archbishop of Dublin in 1719, curate of St Michael's in Dublin, bound for Charleston, South Carolina, in 1734. [FPA.145]

ONGE, ANNE, of Aungier Street, Dublin, married John Staples a Notary Public of the Royal Exchange of London, in 1764. [FDJ.3789]

ONGE, Lieutenant WALTER, died in Luke Street, Dublin, in 1766. [FDJ.4067]

ORD, JOHN, a merchant in Dublin, probate 1656 PCC

OSBORNE, ALEXANDER, in Dublin, a letter, 1685. [PRONI.D1618.2.44]; a minister in Dublin, lately in Ayr, testament, 1690, Commissariat of Edinburgh. [NRS]

OSBORN, JOHN, of the Inner Temple in London, died in Dublin, probate 1694 PCC

OWEN, GEORGE, son of Thomas Owen a silk dyer, died in Meath Street, Dublin, in 1765. [FDJ.3932]

OWENS, PATRICK, a boatman, died on George's Quay, Dublin, in 1764. [FDJ.3929]

OXBROUGH, Colonel HENRY, a Roman Catholic officer in Dublin in 1693. [CSPDom.1693.16]

PADMORE, ARTHUR. in Sheep Street, St Bride's parish, Dublin, 1659. [C]

PAGE, THOMAS, from Dublin, an indentured servant in Philadelphia, Pennsylvania, 1745. [EP.63]

PAGET, MAR., a Fellow of Trinity College, Dublin, in 1618. [CSPIre]

PAGET, THOMAS, formerly a woollen draper in Dublin, died in Carlow in 1766. [FDJ.4079]

PAINE, HARBERT, a lease in Dublin, 1675. [PRONI.D514.3]

PAINE, JOHN, a gentleman in Swan Alley, Dublin, in 1659. [C]

PAINTING, ROBERT, an almsman in Dublin, a petition, 1601? [SPI.1601.647]

PALFERY, RICHARD, a gentleman in Wine Tavern Street, Dublin, 1659. [C]

PALLAS, Captain, a Roman Catholic officer in Dublin in 1693. [CSPDom.1693.16]

PALLEN, ..., a shop-keeper in Francis Street, Dublin, died 1764. [FDJ.3832]

PALMER, CHRISTOPHER, a gentleman in Swan Alley, Dublin, in 1659. [C]

PALMER or COTTON, ELIZABETH, wife of William Palmer in Dublin, will, 1750, refers to her husband, to sister Hannah Davison or Cotton, Edward Fole in Dublin, Mr Throp, Dr Mosse, John Goodwin of the Royal Hospital in Dublin, and his wife, Jane Dalgarno, Robert Robinson a doctor of physics, Christopher Robinson, and to Elizabeth Hansard, all in Dublin; wits. Michael Clarke and Edward Croker an apothecary, boh in Dublin, and Anthony Coane in Strabane. [DRD].

PALMER, HENRY, a mason, was admitted as a Freeman of Dublin in 1654. [DLA]; a mason and a brother of the Corporation of Carpenters in Dublin, 1656. [DCA.G2/1]

PARKER, NATHANIEL, a gentleman in Dublin, will, 1762, refers to his wife Rebecca, their children John, Daniel, Rachel, Rebecca, and Ann, their grandchildren John Gibson and Nathaniel Gibson; wits. Peter Tomey a carpenter in Dolphin's Barn Lane, Dublin, Thomas Barrow a skinner there, and William Dixon NP, and his apprentice George Hughes. [DRD]

PARKER, STEPHEN, a letter-founder in William Street, Dublin, married Miss Thomson of Ross Lane, Dublin, in 1766. [FDJ]

PARKINSON, RICHARD, in Dublin, a deed, 1786. [PRONI.D298.60]

PARNELL, JOHN, in Dublin, letters, 1713. [TCD.750.1457/1466]

PARROT, ..., died in Jervis Street, Dublin, in 1766. [FDJ.4043]

PARRY, JOHN, a publican, died in Hawkin's Street, Dublin, in 1763. [FDJ.3726]

PARSONS, RICHARD, an attorney in Skinner Row, Dublin, married Mrs Perkins of Francis Street, Dublin, in 1766. [FDJ.4107]

PARSONS, Sir WILLIAM, in Dublin, a deed, 1622. [Inchiquin ms1023]

PATTEN, Mrs, widow of Joseph Paten a chandler, died in Charles Street, Dublin, in 1766. [FDJ.4096]

PAYNE, THOMAS, a trunk-maker and a brother of the Corporation of Carpenters in Dublin, 1656. [DCA.G2/1]

PEAKE, JOHN, died at sea aboard the Margaret of Dublin, probate 1678 PCC

PEAKE. MARSHALL, in St Bride's parish, Dublin, in 1659. [C]

PEALL, THOMAS, in Dublin, a letter, 1800. [PRONI.D207.29.27]

PEARCE, ROBERT, in Dublin, 1632. [GAR.ONA.137.363.172]

PEARSON, WILLIAM, died in the George Inn, Golden Lane, Dublin, in 1766. [FDJ.4084]

PEARSON, Mrs, relict of Alderman Pearson, died in Little Cuffe Street, Dublin, in 1764. [FDJ.3831]

PEARSON, Mrs, wife of James Pearson a brazier, died in Chequer Lane, Dublin, in 1764. [FDJ.3818]

PELHAM, Sir EDMUND, Chief Baron of the Exchequer in Dublin, probate 1609 PCC

PELISSIER, ABEL, a Huguenot soldier in the service of King William, died 1727 in Dublin. [HSP.XLI.56]

PELTIER, JAMES, born in Saumur, France, a Huguenot soldier in the service of King William, died 1721 in Dublin. [HSP.XLI.56]

PEMERTON, RICHARD, in Dublin, a lease, 1620. [PRONI.D430.128]

PENDRED, Miss LETITIA, died in Great Cuffe Street, Dublin, in 1766. [FDJ.4075]

PENN, WILLIAM, in Dublin, 1698. [NRS.GD406.1.4318]

PENTENY, EDWARD, in Skinner Row, parish of St Nicholas within the Walls, Dublin, in 1659. [C]

PEPPARD, JACOB, in Dublin, a will, 1747, wife Jane Peppard, son Robert Peppard, Thomas Gonne, and his clerk John Nolan, daughter Dianna Peppard, daughter Elizabeth Barlow, grandson James Barlow, son in law William Barlow, John Stoyte alderman, Thomas Cooke NP and his clerk George More. [DRD]

PEPYS, MARY, a widow in Dublin, probate 1660 PCC

PERCIVALL, CHRISTOFER, a merchant in Dublin, probate 1606 PCC

PERCIVAL, JOHN, in Dublin, leases, 1664/1697. [PRONI.D430.170; D971.34.A72]

PERCIVAL, Reverend KANE, minister of the parish of St Michans, Dublin, a letter from George Brereton at the Hanoverian camp in Inverness, 26 April 1746. [PRONI.D906.85]

PERCIVAL, Dr ROBERT, in Dublin, a marriage settlement, 1785. [PRONI.D906.18]

PERKINS, JOHN, a gentleman in Dublin, will, 1766, refers to Francis Harvey in Dublin, and John Fenn in Johnstown, County Dublin, his brother Theophilus Perkins and his cousin Theophilus Perkins; wits. William Harvey, Thornton Francis Ryan, James Hornidge, gentlemen in Dublin, William Cotton a linen draper and Joseph Waddy, both gentlemen in Dublin. [DRD]

PERRY, EDMUND, in Dublin, a letter, 1783. [PRONI.D1606.1.1.103]

PETERS, WALTER, in Dublin, probate 1692

PETRY, JEAN, from Heidelberg, Germany, a Huguenot soldier in the service of King William, probate 1723 Dublin

PETTIT, WILLIAM, servant to James Bedlowe a merchant and Alderman of Dublin, a declaration, 1601.[SPI.1601.190]

PHELAN, Lieutenant ANDREW, a Roman Catholic officer in Dublin in 1693. [CSPDom.1693.16]

PHEPOE, RICHARD, from Dublin, was naturalised in South Carolina in 1796. [NARA.M1183]

PHILLIPS, COLLEY, Searcher and Gauger of the port of Dublin in 1626. [CPRIre]

PHILPOT, WILLIAM, a merchant in Dublin, was admitted as a burgess and guilds-brother of Glasgow in 1724. [GBR]

PHIPPES, PEN, a senior fellow of Trinity College, Dublin, 1661. [CSPIre]

PIERCE, MARK, in London, died in Dublin, probate 1656 PCC

PIERCE, WILLIAM, in Westenra's, Bridge Street, Dublin, a letter, 1664. [PRONI.T2929.1.2.4]

PIERREFRITE, JUDITH, from Vendome, France, died 1710 in Dublin, wife of Daniel de la Fontan. [HSP.XLI.38]

PIKEMAN, JOHN, a Fellow of Trinity College, Dublin, in 1618. [CSPIre]

PIN, JOHN, in Skinner Row, parish of St Nicholas within the Walls, Dublin, in 1659. [C]

PINSON, JOHN, in St Bride's parish, Dublin, in 1659. [C]

PIPPARD, Captain CHRISTOPHER, a Roman Catholic officer in Dublin in 1693. [CSPDom.1693.16]

PIPPARD, THOMAS, in Dublin, a deed, 1637. [PRONI.D1741.1]

PITT, ANNE, in Dublin, a will, 1755, refers to her uncle ....Skerrett, her aunt Susanna Flack, and William Powell an apothecary; wits. Randall

Slack, Christopher Rice a cutler, and William Cosgrave a merchant, and Thomas Biggs, all in Dublin. [DRD]

PITT, JOHN, in Dublin, a lease, 1620. [PRONI.D430.128]; in Skinner Row, parish of St Nicholas within the Walls, Dublin, in 1659. [C]

PITTMAN, ELIZABETH, a Methodist in Dublin, died 1791

PLAYFORD, Captain, in Sheep Street, St Bride's parish, Dublin, 1659. [C]

PLUNKETT, GEORGE, a merchant in Dublin, a pardon in 1608. [HMC.31]

PLUNKETT, WALTER, in Dublin, a deed, 1656. [PRONI.T956.28]

PLUNKETT, Mr, a brewer in Ann Street, near the Linen Hall, Dublin, died in 1764. [FDJ.3842]

POCKLINGTON, Admiral, died in Grafton Street, Dublin, in 1766. [FDJ.4121]

POMEROY, HENRY, in Dublin, a letter, 1793. [PRONI.T2541.1B.3.4.6]

PONSONBY, JOHN, in Dublin, a letter, 1781. [PRONI.D207.67.2]

PONTY, JAMES, a brazier in Back Lane, Dublin, died in 1764. [FDJ.3844]

POOLY, THOMAS, in Damask Street, St Andrews parish, Dublin, in 1659. [C]

POOLEY, Mrs, wife of William Pooley, died in Malpas Street, Dublin, in 1764. [FDJ.3814]

POOPE, THOMAS, in St Bride's parish, Dublin, in 1659. [C]

POPE, Mrs, died on Milltown Road, Dublin, in 1766. [FDJ.4128]

PORTAL, JEAN, a Huguenot soldier in the service of King William, died 1737 in Dublin. [HSP.XLI.58]

POTTER, WILLIAM, a bricklayer, was admitted as a Freeman of Dublin in 1649. [DLA]

POTTER, WILLIAM, a mason and a brother of the Corporation of Carpenters in Dublin, 1656. [DCA.G2/1]

POTTER, Captain, and WALTER POTTER his son, in St Bride's parish, Dublin, in 1659. [C]

POULTER, ANTHONY, a member of the Guild of Brewers in Dublin, 1669. [CSPIre]

POWELL, FLEETWOOD, a merchant in Temple Lane, Dublin, died in 1764. [FDJ.3846]

POWELL, HUGH, a blacksmith from Dublin, an indentured servant bound for Barbados in 1698. [LRO]

POWELL, SAMUEL, jr., born 1743, died in Dame Street, Dublin, 1766. [FDJ.4101]

PRATT, Captain JOHN, in Dublin, letters, 1706-1709. [PRONI.D638.168.1-8]

PRATT, JOHN, in Dublin, a deed, 1730. [PRONI.D207.21]

PRESCOTT, ..., in King Street, Dublin, married Catherine Groves of Hawkin Street, Dublin, in 1770. [FLJ.50]

PRESTON, JOHN, in Skinner Row, parish of St Nicholas within the Walls, Dublin, in 1659. [C]

PRESTON, THOMASINA BARNEWELL MARY ANTHONY, in Dublin, a bond, 1697. [PRONI.D1044.844]

PRESTON, ..., son of John Preston MP, was born in St Stephen's Green, Dublin, in 1764. [FDJ.3812]

PRICE, Mrs MARY, died in Britain Street, Dublin, 1763. [FDJ.3727]

PRICE, OWEN, a merchant in Dublin, probate 1683 PCC

PRICE, THOMAS, a soldier from Dublin, died in London, probate 1674 PCC

PRIOU, JEAN, born 1653, a Huguenot soldier in the service of King William, died in Dublin 1703. [HSP.XLI.59]

PRITCHET, Captain, in Golden Lane, St Bride's parish, Dublin, 1659. [C]

PROCTOR, THOMAS, a cooper in Dublin, a will, 1776, refers to his son-in-law James Rochfort in Dublin, James Lambe a merchant in Dublin, his grandson Thomas Rochfort, his granddaughter Elizabeth – daughter of Alice Fox; wits. Thomas Hackett a victualler in Dublin, Thomas Hutton a victualler in Dublin, Thomas Downing a grocer in Dublin, and Bartholomew O'Brian. [DRD]

PURCELL, RICHARD, an apothecary in Dublin, a lease in Cork Street, Dublin, in 1683. [PRONI.D3078.1.20.4]

PURCELL, Captain RICHARD, a Roman Catholic officer in Dublin in 1693. [CSPDom.1693.16]

PURDON, JOHN, an Attorney of H M Court of the Exchequer, married Anne Nixon of Longford, in 1764. [FDJ.3809]

PUREFOY, BAZILL, a member of the Guild of Brewers in Dublin, 1669. [CSPIre]

PUREFOY, JAMES, a merchant, former apprentice to William Snell, was admitted as a Freeman of Dublin in 1686. [DLA]

PURSLOW, JOHN, a husbandman from Dublin, emigrated to Pennsylvania in 1677. [EP.21]

PYNE, RICHARD, a linen draper in Bride Street, Dublin, married Miss Winterbottom of Usher's Quay, Dublin, in 1766. [FDJ.4053]

QUIN, LAURENCE, and Peggy Hatton, both of Kildare Street, Dublin, married in 1766. [FDJ.4131]

QUIRK, THOMAS, in Dublin, a bond, 1648. [PRONI.D430.154]; a maltster, was admitted as a Freeman of Dublin in 1648. [DLA]

QUOYLE, PATRICK, a cooper and a member of the Fraternity of St Patrick's near Dublin in 1666. [CalSPIre]

RABITEAU, Mrs, wife of John Charles Rabiteau a merchant, died in Nicholas Street, Dublin, in 1764. [FDJ.3832]

RADCLIFFE, GEORGE, in Dublin, 1639. [NRS.GD504.9.97]

RADCLIFFE, ..., son of Stephen Radcliffe a Counsellor at Law, was born in Bride Street, Dublin, in 1764. [FDJ.3829]

RAGGE, WILLIAM, a miller, was admitted as a Freeman of Dublin in 1651, [DLA]; a miller and a brother of the Corporation of Carpenters in Dublin, 1656. [DCA.G2/1]

RAINBUCK, THOMAS, a cooper and a member of the Fraternity of St Patrick's near Dublin in 1666. [CalSPIre]

RALFE, CATHERINE, a petition on behalf of the poor widows of Thomas Street, Dublin, 1711. [TNA.SP34.32.12]

RAM, WILLIAM, a carpenter and a brother of the Corporation of Carpenters in Dublin, 1656. [DCA.G2/1]

RAMSEY, EDMOND, in Skinner Row, parish of St Nicholas within the Walls, Dublin, in 1659. [C]

RANKIN, Mrs, wife of John Rankin a printer, died in Mary's Street, Dublin, in 1766. [FDJ.4057]

RAVENSCROFT, JOHN, a joiner and a brother of the Corporation of Carpenters in Dublin, 1656. [DCA.G2/1]

RAWLINS, JOSEPH, a merchant, was admitted as a Freeman of Dublin in 1754, [DLA]; a stuff manufacturer in Francis Street, Dublin, died in 1766. [FDJ.4081]

THE PEOPLE OF DUBLIN, 1600-1799

READ, JOHN and HANNAH, in Dublin, a lease, 1694. [PRONI.D2538.A20]

READ, RICHARD, a dealer in Back Lane, Dublin, will, 1748, wife Phillis Lennox or Read, his brother William Read and his children Mathew, Katherine, and Dina, his brother James Read and his daughters; John Clark a chandler, wits Murray Kathrens, and Lucy Read, all in Dublin. [DRD]

READE, Captain THOMAS, a Roman Catholic officer in Dublin in 1693. [CSPDom.1693.16]

READ, Master WILLIAM, son of John Read a cutler in Dublin, died 1766. [FDJ.4066]

READING, BENJAMIN, in Pelletstown, Dublin, will, 1771, refers to his friend Barry Colles in Dublin, Rebecca Tomly wife of William Read a master porter on Aston's Quay, Mrs Mary Gumly; wits. William Smart a writing clerk in Dublin, Patrick Conlan a writing clerk in Dublin, Patrick Butler a grocer in Michael's Lane, Dublin, William Fleming a peruke maker in Christ Church lane, Dublin, Peter Dillon a weaver in the Combe, William Costello in Dublin clerk to Barry Colles, and Edward George a gentleman in Dublin. [DRD]

READING, ROBERT, in Dublin, died 8 January 1764, will, 1764, refers to friends in Dublin – Michael Chamberlain and Barry Colles, his sister Elenor Reading or Coughlan, his brother Benjamin Reading. Wits. Richard Jackson DL, Franklin Drury, Constantine Cullen the Registrar of the High Court of Chancery, and William Costello, all in Dublin, [DRD]

REASON, WILLIAM, a bricklayer and a brother of the Corporation of Carpenters in Dublin, 1656. [DCA.G2/1]

REDMAN, ANNE, in Dublin, 1665. [NRS.GD406.1.10012]

REED, ..., master of the Ceres of Dublin trading with Madeira and St Kitts in 1764. [DJ:19.5.1764]

REILLY, JOHN, from Dublin, an indentured servant in Philadelphia, Pennsylvania, 1745. [EP.55]

REILLY, Mrs MARGARET, wife of Michael Reilly a merchant, died on Lazer's Hill, Dublin, in 1766. [FDJ.4061]

REILLY, THOMAS, a mason and a brother of the Corporation of Carpenters in Dublin, 1656. [DCA.G2/1]

REILLY, Mrs, wife of John Reilly a watchmaker, died in Crampton Court, Dublin, in 1764. [FDJ.3781]

RELY, JAMES, a gentleman in Dublin, a deed, 1686. [Inchiquin ms1211]

RETSON, ROBERT, a bricklayer and a brother of the Corporation of Carpenters in Dublin, 1656. [DCA.G2/1]

REYNOLDS, CHARLES, born 1770, a shoemaker from Dublin, was naturalised in South Carolina in 1802. [NARA.M1183]

REYNOLDS, EDWARD, of Francis Street, Dublin, married Miss Andrews of Castle Street, Dublin, in 1766. [FDJ.4056]

REYNOLDS, FRANCIS, a baker in Dublin, died in 1766. [FDJ.4047]

REYNOLDS, Mrs, wife of Andrew Reynolds, died in Ash Street, Dublin, in 1764. [FDJ.3924]

RHODES, SAMUEL, a merchant in Dublin, 'died beyond the seas', probate 1653 PCC

RICE, Sir STEPHEN, in Dublin, a lease, 1692. [Inchiquin ms 1223]

RICHARD, ..., in St Bride's parish, Dublin, in 1659. [C]

RICHARDS, Mr, a surveyor, died in Abbey Street, Dublin, in 1766. [FDJ.4054]

RICHARDSON, ARCHIBALD, surgeon to the State, married Hanna Dawson of Dorset Street, Dublin, in 1766. [FDJ.4136]

THE PEOPLE OF DUBLIN, 1600-1799

RICHARDSON, JOHN, in Dublin, a letter, 1617. [PRONI.D683.31]

RICHARDSON, MIDDLETON, a carpenter, was admitted as a Freeman of Dublin in 1654, [DLA]; a carpenter and a brother of the Corporation of Carpenters in Dublin, 1656. [DCA.G2/1]

RICHARDSON, ROBERT, an apothecary, was admitted as a Freeman of Dublin in 1690, [DLA]; an apothecary in Dublin, a lease, 1694. [PRONI.D2538.A20]

RICE, THOMAS, in Dublin, lease of silver mines, 1706. [PRONI.D623.B6.11]

RICH, Captain, a gentleman in Lazy Hill, College Green, Dublin, in 1659. [C]

RICHARDSON, ARCHIBALD, a lease, 1780. [PRONI.D300.2.1.126/2]; a will, 1787. [PRONI.D300.1.59]

RICHT, ... |a gentleman in St Bride's parish, Dublin, in 1659. [C]

RIDGES, WILLIAM, a former Customs Collector in Dublin, 1659. [CSPIre]

RISK, JOHN, a painter and a Methodist in Dublin, died 1792.

ROATH, Captain, a Roman Catholic officer in Dublin in 1693. [CSPDom.1693.16]

ROBERTS, EDWARD, in Stevens Street, Dublin, 1659. [C]

ROBERTS, NATHANIEL, a bricklayer and a brother of the Corporation of Carpenters in Dublin, 1656. [DCA.G2/1]

ROBERTSON, ANTHONY, a watchmaker in Dublin, a commission, 1777. [NRAS.2522.CA4.1.74]

ROBERTSON, ARCHIBALD, a physician in Dublin, a letter, 1784. [PRONI.D207.20.49]

123

THE PEOPLE OF DUBLIN, 1600-1799

ROBERTSON, WILLIAM, from Dublin, a soldier in Dutch service, bound from the Netherlands to the West Indies aboard the White Swan, an inventory, 1638. [Old Notarial Accounts. Rotterdam Inventories.293]

ROBINS, THOMAS, a merchant in Dublin, was admitted as a burgess and guilds-brother of Glasgow in 1724. [GBR]

ROBINSON, ANN, a widow in Dublin, will, 1750, brother John Jackson a clerk, cousin Reverend Daniel Jackson a clerk, James Grattan, sisters Jane and Frances Jackson; wits. Catherine Gunning, Robert Robinson, Francis Evans, and Peter Shee a merchant, all in Dublin. [DRD]

ROBINSON, GEORGE, a painter in Dublin, a petition, 1761. [PRONI.D207.23.1]

ROBINSON, RICHARD, a distiller and a brother of the Corporation of Carpenters in Dublin, 1656. [DCA.G2/1]

ROBINSON, ROBERT, a farrier, married Mrs Kennedy on the Strand, Dublin, in 1770. [FLJ.53]

ROBINSON, WILLIAM, a plasterer, was admitted as a Freeman of Dublin in 1655, [DLA]; a plasterer and a brother of the Corporation of Carpenters in Dublin, 1656. [DCA.G2/1]

ROBINSON WILLIAM, a brazier in Castle Street, Dublin, died 1766. [FDJ.4045]

ROBINSON, WILLIAM, born 1772 in Dublin, naturalised in South Carolina in 1808. [NARA.M1183]

ROBINSON, ..., daughter of Robert Robinson MD, died in Sackville Street, Dublin, in 1766. [FDJ.4120]

ROCHE, Mrs, widow of Richard Roche, died in Phrapper Lane, Dublin, in 1766. [FDJ.4079]

ROCHE, ..., master of the Earl of Dublin trading with Philadelphia in 1784. [PaMercury,7]

124

ROCHFORD, JOHN, a cutler and a member of the Guild of St Luke the Evangelist in Dublin in 1669. [CSPIre]

ROCHFORD, ROBERT, in Backhouse Lane, Dublin, 1692, [CTB.IX.1708]; in Dublin, a deed, 1694. [PRONI.D74.1]

ROE, ANTHONY, a gentleman in St George's Lane, parish of St Andrew, Dublin, in 1659. [C]

ROE, JANE, in Dublin, widow of Dr William Roe, will 1749, son Andrew Roe, daughter Mary Walsh, grand-daughter Jane Walsh, grand-daughter Jane Cane wife of William Despard in Dublin, sister Ann Le Singe, son in law Phillip Walsh; wits John King, Nathaniel Smith a woollen draper, and Henry Duggan a tailor, all in Dublin. [DRD]

ROGERS, JOHN, a carpenter, was admitted as a Freeman of Dublin in 1651. [DLA]; a carpenter and a brother of the Corporation of Carpenters in Dublin, 1656. [DCA.G2/1]

ROGERSON, FRANCIS, a carpenter, was admitted as a Freeman of Dublin in 1653. [DLA]; a carpenter and a brother of the Corporation of Carpenters in Dublin, 1656. [DCA.G2/1]

ROIFFE, JEAN, from Chattellerault, Vienne, France, a Huguenot soldier in the service of King William, died in Dublin in 1726. [HSP.XLI.61]

ROLLS, SAMUEL, a doctor of medicine in Dublin, died in London, probate 1691 PCC

RONEY, Cornet, in Golden Lane, St Bride's parish, Dublin, 1659. [C]

ROONEY, JAMES, in Dublin, a letter, 1756. [PRONI.D619.21N.160]

ROSE, EDWARD, a merchant, was admitted as a Freeman of Dublin in 1681, [DRD]; a merchant in Dublin, probate 1699 PCC

ROSE, WILLIAM, Adjutant to the Royal Hospital in Dublin, QM of the Royal Irish Dragoons during the wars of Queen Anne serving abroad with great distinction, later served under King George I and King George II, died in the Royal Hospital in 1764. [FDJ.3806]

ROSS, DANIEL, master of the brig Dolly of Dublin trading with Virginia in 1789. [PIG.124 4/1252]

ROSS, JAMES, a victualler in Cherry Lane, Dublin, will, 1752, wife Catherine Ross, daughter Anne Ross, Patrick Horish a chandler, Patrick White, wits. Thomas Philpott, Christopher Dalton NP, and his clerk William Williams, all in Dublin. [DRD]

ROSS, JOHN, Curate of St Ann's, died at St Stephen's Green, Dublin, in 1763. [FDJ.3725]

ROSS, ROBERT, master of the Dublin Merchant in 1699. [Admiralty Court of Virginia]

ROTHERY, WILLIAM, a mason in Dublin, a lease of Cork Street, Dublin, in 1683. [PRONI.D3078.1.20.4]

ROURKE, ..., a hatter in Meath Street, Dublin, died in 1766. [FDJ.4114]

ROW, HENRY, a shoemaker in Dublin, was denizised in Ireland in 1666. [IPR]; was admitted as a Freeman of Dublin in 1676. [DLA]

ROWAN, ELIZABETH, a widow in Dublin, a deed, 1773. [PRONI.130.1]

ROWAN, WILLIAM, in Dublin, a lease, 1734. [PRONI.D110.1]

ROWLEY, CLOTWORTHY, in Dublin, a deed, 1789. [PRONI.D313.10]

ROWLEY, JAMES, a slater in James Street, Dublin, a will, 1773, refers to his son John Rowley and his son's wife Elinor, his grandson James Mckilwaine, wits. Robert Beven a gentleman in Bason Lane, Dublin, Peter Wilkinson a weaver in James Street, Dublin, George Ledgwick a girt weaver in James Street, Dublin, and Michael Macabe a gentleman in Dublin. [DRD]; was admitted as a Freeman of Dublin in 1758. [DLA]

ROYDON, MATTHEW, in Dublin, probate 1676 PCC

RUISHE, Sir FRANCIS, in Dublin, probate 1623 PCC

RUSSELL, JOHN, in Dublin in 1639. [GAR.ONA.145.204.415]

RUSSELL, JOHN, in Castle Street, Dublin, died in 1766. [FDJ.4111]

RUSSELL, Captain THOMAS, a Roman Catholic officer in Dublin in 1693. [CSPDom.1693.16]

RUSSELL, THOMAS, and the widow McManus, both of George's Quay, Dublin, were married in 1770. [FLJ.53]

RUSSELL, Captain WILLIAM, a Roman Catholic officer in Dublin in 1693. [CSPDom.1693.16]

RYAN, Captain DARBY, a Roman Catholic officer in Dublin in 1693. [CSPDom.1693.16]

RYAN, JOHN, a felt-maker, was admitted as a Freeman of Dublin in 1729. [DLA]

RYAN, ROBERT, a tailor, son of Joseph Ryan, was admitted as a Freeman of Dublin in 1758. [DLA]

RYAN, TIMOTHY, from Dublin, an indentured servant in Philadelphia, Pennsylvania, 1745. [EP.56]

RYLEY, Major HUGH, a Roman Catholic officer in Dublin in 1693. [CSPDom.1693.16]

RYLEY, Lieutenant, a Roman Catholic officer in Dublin in 1693. [CSPDom.1693.16]

ST FERREOL, PAUL, a French minister, lately in Hamburg, now 'under call to a French congregation in Dublin', was admitted as a burgess and guilds-brother of Glasgow in 1717. [GBR]

THE PEOPLE OF DUBLIN, 1600-1799

ST GEORGE, OLIVER, in Dublin, a will, 1695. [PRONI.D1932.8.23]

ST GEORGE, ..., son of Richard St George of Kilrush, was born in Kildare Street, Dublin, in 1766. [FDJ.4051]

ST LEGER, ARTHUR, in Dublin, a deed, 1692. [PRONI.D509.31]

ST LEGER, MARY, in Dublin, a deed, 1692. [PRONI.D509.31]

SALLY, Captain EDMUND, a Roman Catholic officer in Dublin in 1693. [CSPDom.1693.16]

SAMFORD, RICHARD, a cooper and a member of the Fraternity of St Patrick's near Dublin in 1666. [CalSPIre]

SAMPSON, JANE, widow of Michael Sampson, died in Dominick Street, Dublin, in 1764. [FDJ.3831]

SANDERSON, JOHN, a plumber and a brother of the Corporation of Carpenters in Dublin, 1656. [DCA.G2/1]

SANDFORD, JOHN, born 1780, a grocer from Dublin, naturalised in Charleston, South Carolina, in 1814. [NARA.M1183]

SANDS, ELIZABETH, born 1691, relict of Joseph Sands, died in Bride Street, Dublin, in 1764. [FDJ.3788]

SANDS, Sir WILLIAM, in Dublin, probate 1687 PCC

SANDYS, Mrs ANN, wife of Rev. Michael Sandys, died in Grafton Street, Dublin, in 1764. [FDJ.3844]

SANFORD, the widow, married William Forster of Dunleer, County Louth, in Capel Street, Dublin, in 1764. [FDJ.3809]

SANKEY, HENRY, in Sheep Street, St Bride's parish, Dublin, 1659. [C]

SANKEY, RICHARD, in Dublin, a lease, 1695. [PRONI.D778.17]

SANKEY, THOMAS, town major of the garrison in Dublin, 1771. [CHOP.1771.984]

SARSFIELD, JOHN, a cutler and a member of the Guild of St Luke the Evangelist in Dublin, 1669. [CSPIre]

SAULE, ..., in St Thomas Street, Dublin, 1585. [CBP.II.1227]

SAUNDERS, ARTHUR, of Trinity College, was admitted as a Freeman of Belfast in 1753. [TBB]

SAUNDERS, GEORGE, a jeweller, died in Capel Street, Dublin, in 1766. [FDJ.4078]

SAURIN DE MARRAUL, ETIENNE, from Guienne, France, a Huguenot soldier in the service of King William, settled in Dublin, died 1741 and buried in St Patrick's. [HSP.XLI.65]

SAUSINESS, DOMINICK, master of the Mary of Dublin, trading with San Sebastian in Spain, 1693. [CTB.XIX.246]

SAVAGE, EDWARD, a merchant in Dublin, was admitted as a burgess and guilds-brother of Ayr in 1743. [ABR]

SAVAGE, JOHN, in Dublin, a will, 1711, [PRONI.D662]

SAVAGE, PHILIP, in Dublin, deeds, 1667, [NAI.2000.20.4.1]; 1692. [PRONI.D552.B1.1.84]

SAVAGE, ROWLAND, in Dublin, a mortgage, 1676. [PRONI.D552.B1.1.66]

SAWKILL, Mr, of Pill Lane, Dublin, married Sally Ireland of High Street, Dublin, in 1764. [FDJ.3806]

SCANLAN, JOHN, a shoemaker in Bride Street, Dublin, died 1766. [FDJ.4065]

SCOTT, ROBERT, a cooper, was admitted as a Freeman of Dublin in 1662, [DLA]; a cooper and a member of the Fraternity of St Patrick's near Dublin in 1666. [CalSPIre]

SCURLOCK, THOMAS, a soldier and Freeman of New York, brother of Mary Scurlock or Karby in Dublin, probate 1747 in New York.

SEADON, RANDALPH, a butcher in St Patrick Street, Dublin, was denisized in Ireland in 1665. [IPR]; a butcher, was admitted as a Freeman of Dublin in 1676. [DLA]

SEAMAN, CALEB, a carpenter and a brother of the Corporation of Carpenters in Dublin, 1656. [DCA.G2/1]; was admitted as a Freeman of Dublin in 1656. [DLA]

SEAMAN, ROBERT, in St Bride's parish, Dublin, in 1659. [C]

SEDEN, WILLIAM. in Sheep Street, St Bride's parish, Dublin, 1659. [C]

SEDGRAVE, ANNE, in High Street, Dublin, 1626. [CPRIre]

SEDGRAVE, WALTER, in High Street, Dublin, 1626. [CPRIre]

SEELE, THOMAS, provost of Trinity College, Dublin, 1661. [CSPIre]

SEGUELA, ETIENNE, from Bergerac, France, a Huguenot soldier in the service of King William, died in Dublin in 1727. [HSP.XLI.66]

SEGUIN, ..., a sugar baker in George's Lane, Dublin, died 1764. [FDJ.3832]

SERGEANT, JOHN, master of the brigantine Union of Dublin bound for Jamaica and Philadelphia, Pennsylvania, in 1752. [VaGaz.81]

SEVE, ETIENNE, born 1631, a Huguenot soldier in the service of King William, died in Dublin in 1707. [HSP.XLI.66]

SEVER, THOMAS, in Dublin, a deposition, 1641. [PRONI.D1923.1.16B]

SEXTEN, GEORGE, in Dublin, a letter, 1607. [PRONI.D778.1A]

SHANE, Captain FRANCIS, in St Bride's parish, Dublin, in 1659. [C]

SHARPLEY, WILLIAM, a cabinet maker in Clarendon Street, Dublin, died in 1766. [FDJ.4098]

SHAUGHNES, Mrs MARIE, widow of John Shaugnes in Dublin, lease of a house on High Street, Dublin, in 1614. [PRONI.D430.118-119]

SHAW, PATRICK, in Dublin, a letter, 1710. [PRONI.D562.87]

SHAW, ROBERT, in Dublin Castle, a letter, 1789. [PRONI.D561.8092]

SHAW, WILLIAM, in Dublin, a letter, 1694. [PRONI.D778.16]

SHAW, Captain, in St Bride's parish, Dublin, in 1659. [C]

SHEA, ROBERT, married Miss Bellew of Usher's Quay, Dublin, in 1764. [FDJ.3820]

SHEAL, RICHARD, a vintner in Liffey Street, Dublin, died in 1766. [FDJ.4081]

SHEALE, TOBY, in Dublin, a deed, 1637. [PRONI.D1741.1]

SHEAPHEARD, JOHN, a gentleman in Fishamble Street, St John's parish, Dublin, in 1659. [C]

SHEHY, CHARLES, an indentured servant from Dublin, bound for America in 1698. [LRO]

SHELTON, JOHN, in Dublin, 1602. [SPI.1602.400]

SHELTON, THOMAS, in Dublin, a lease, 1647. [PRONI.D430.151]

SHEPERD, GABRIEL, a clothier in Dublin, a Quaker, will, 1745 Dublin

SHERLOCK, BALSHAZAR, master of the Thomas of Dublin seized by Customs at Glendere in Ireland in 1705. [CTB.XIX.543]

SHERWIN, JOHN, a goldsmith, was admitted as a Freeman of Dublin in 1658, [DLA]; a goldsmith in Skinner's Row, Dublin, married the widow Kavenagh of Peter Street, Dublin, in 1765. [FDJ.3932]

THE PEOPLE OF DUBLIN, 1600-1799

SHERWOOD, JOHN, will, 1759, Dublin. [PRONI.T1075.37]

SHIMIN, ROBERT, a wine merchant in Bridgefoot Street, Dublin, died in 1766. [FDJ.4073]

SHIRLEY, NICHOLAS, died at the widow Grattan's in Marlborough Street, Dublin, in 1764. [FDJ.3826]

SHURLOG, Sir THOMAS, and his son James, in Skinner Row, parish of St Nicholas within the Walls, Dublin, in 1659. [C]

SIBBALD, JAMES, a Presbyterian minister in Dublin before 1647. [F.7.533]

SILCOCK, GABRIEL, a glazier, son of Galriel Silcock, was admitted as a Freeman of Dublin in 1747. [DLA]

SILCOCK, ..., a glazier in Dublin, died in 1766. [FDJ.4046]

SIMPSON, RICHARD, in Dublin, a charter party re a voyage from Dublin to Stockholm, Sweden, in 1726. [PRONI.D354.389]

SKELTON, SAMUEL, died in Bride Street, Dublin, in 1765. [FDJ.3936]

SLEIGH, JOSEPH, a tanner in Dublin, a Quaker, probate 1683 Dublin

SLICER, EDWARD, a jeweller in Dublin, will, 1753, son Samuel Slicer, daughters Ann Paine and Mary Shaw, grand-daughter Ann Rouse; wits. Christopher Dalton NP, and his clerks William Williams and Mark Gerrard, in Dublin. [DRD]

SMITH, ANN, wife of William Smith a coach-maker, died in Great Britain Street, Dublin, in 1766. [FDJ.4113]

SMITH, FRANCIS, and MARY WHELAN or SMITH, in St James Street, Dublin, a deed, 1786. [PRONI.D298.56]

SMITH, JAMES, in Dublin, will, 1746, wife Ruth Smith, sons John Smith, Edward Smith, wits Redmond Boate surgeon, Joseph Kathrens, and Timothy Green yeoman, Rev. Richard Ratcliffe, all in Dublin. [DRD]

SMITH, JOHN, from Dublin, 'died beyond the seas', probate 1653 PCC

SMITH, NICHOLAS, from Dublin, an indentured servant in Philadelphia, Pennsylvania, in 1745. [EP.54]

SMITH, WILLIAM, in Dublin, probate 1623 PCC

SMITH, WILLIAM, a servant to John Smith in Dublin, was admitted as a burgess and freeman of Ayr in 1735. [ABR]

SMITH, ..., master of the Nancy of Dublin trading with Virginia in 1751. [VaGaz.7]

SMYTHE, ROBERT, in Dublin, a letter, 1706. [PRONI.D638.43]

SMYTH, Lieutenant WALTER, a Roman Catholic officer in Dublin in 1693. [CSPDom.1693.16]

SMYTH, WILLIAM, an Alderman of Dublin in 1660, [CSPIre]; in Dublin, a lease, 1670. [PRONI.T2125.12.4]

SMYTH, WILLIAM, in Dublin, a deed, 1776. [PRONI.D462.22]

SNEYD, EDWARD, a merchant in Dublin, married Hannah King, at Elphin in 1764. [FDJ.3837]

SOMERS, SAMUEL, a Quaker and a merchant in Meath Street, Dublin, died in 1762. [FDJ.3723]

SOMERTON, Lady J., in Dublin, a letter, 1800. [PRONI.D572.8.48]

SOMERVILL, JAMES, in Dublin, letters, 1701. [TCD.750.779/793/798/803/813]

SOMERVILLE, WILLIAM, a barber in Dublin, was admitted as a burgess and guilds-brother of Glasgow in 1717. [GBR]

SOTHERBY, JOHN, in Dublin, a deed, 1720. [PRONI.D279]

SOUTHERN, FRANCIS, a member of the Guild of Brewers in Dublin in 1669. [CSPIre]

SOUTHERN, JOSEPH, a chandler, was admitted as a Freeman of Dublin in 1676. [DLA]

SPEAR, RICHARD, a merchant in Francis Street, Dublin, married Elizabeth Finchley from Kenagh, County Longford, in 1764. [FDJ.3930]

SPENCER, MICHAEL, an attorney in Dublin, 1720. [NRAS.88.3.71]

SPENCER, WILLIAM, a coachman in Dublin Castle, probate 1695 PCC

STAMPER, GRACE, a widow in Dublin, probate 1679 PCC

STANFORD, Mrs, died in Crow Street, Dublin, in 1766. [FDJ.4050]

STANLEY, RICHARD, a cooper and a member of the Fraternity of St Patrick's near Dublin in 1666. [CalSPIre]

STANLEY, ROBERT, a cooper, former apprentice of Joseph Cook, was admitted as a Freeman of Dublin in 1755. [DLA]

STANLEY, WALTER, a merchant, son of Edward Stanley a merchant, was admitted as a Freeman of Dublin in 1633. [DLA]

STANLEY, Mrs, wife of John Stanley a saddler, died in Castle Street, Dublin, in 1764. [FDJ.3820]

STANTON, RICHARD, in Chequer Lane, Dublin, in 1659. [C]

STAPLES, HENRY, a clerk in Dublin, died in Essex, probate 1687 PCC

STAPLES, ..., son of John Staples in Dominick Street, Dublin, was born in 1766. [FDJ.4046]

STAPLETON, BRYAN, in Dublin, a mortgage, 1720. [PRONI.D671.D11.1.1.]

STAYS, JOHN, master of the Bachelor's Delight of Dublin trading with Madeira and Charleston, South Carolina, in 1732. [TNA.CO5.509]

STEARNE, JOHN, senior fellow of Trinity College, Dublin, 1661. [CSPIre]

STEEL, RALPH, of Dame Street, Dublin, married Jane Wallin of Fleet Street, Dublin, in 1764. [FDJ.3930]

STEELE, SARAH, in Dublin, a mortgage, 1762. [PRONI.D282.20]

STERNE, HENRY, Vestry Clerk of St Werburgh's, died in Cole Alley, Castle Street, Dublin, in 1766. [FDJ.4086]

STEWARD, JAMES, in Skinner Row, parish of St Nicholas within the Walls, Dublin, in 1659. [C]

STEWART, ALEXANDER, a printer, was admitted as a Freeman of Dublin in 1774. [DLA]

STEWART, DONALD, in Dublin, a letter, 1807. [PRONI.D562.12219]

STEWART, GEORGE, in Dublin, a deed, 1682. [PRONI.D552.B1.1.78]

STEWART, JOHN, in Dublin, a lease, 1788. [PRONI.D32.4]

STEWART, THOMAS, a merchant in Pill Lane, Dublin, son of James Stewart, was admitted as a Freeman of Dublin in 1807.[DLA]

STEWART, WALTER, a cooper, was admitted as a Freeman of Dublin in 1609.[DLA]

STEWART, WILLIAM, a barber surgeon, was admitted as a Freeman of Dublin in 1712.[DLA]

STEWART, ..., master of the Thomas of Dublin a brig, from Barbados, was wrecked near Cork on 5 September 1766.

STEWART, Mrs, wife of William Stewart, and daughter of Sir Richard Butler, died in Stafford Street, Dublin, in 1764. [FDJ.3832]

STONE, RICHARD, in Dublin, a lease, 1647. [PRONI.D430.151]

STONE, Mr, a coachmaker, and Miss Ledsom, both in James's Street, Dublin, married in 1766. [FDJ.4130]

STORTON, THOMAS, in Skinner Row, parish of St Nicholas within the Walls, Dublin, in 1659. [C]

STOTTESBURY, LISLE, at The Swan, Fish-shambles Street, Dublin, 1669. [NRS.GD406.1.9863]

STOUGHTON, JOHN, in Sheep Street, St Bride's parish, Dublin, 1659. [C]

STOUGHTON, WILLIAM, in Dublin, a lease, 1630. [PRONI.D430.135]

STRETTELL, AMOS, in Back Lane, Dublin, a deed, 1698; in Dublin, a letter, 1702. [PRONI.D645.5; D562.84]

STRONG, Mrs, wife of Thomas Strong a shoemaker in Mary's Lane, Dublin, died in 1766. [FDJ.4047]

STRONG, Reverend, a Dissenting minister, died in Dublin in 1766. [FDJ.4141]

STRYNY, SILVANUS, in Sheep Street, St Bride's parish, Dublin, 1659. [C]

SULLIVAN, FRANCES, of Crow Street, Dublin, married James Medlicoat Flack, an attorney, in 1764. [FDJ.3788]

SULLIVAN, FRANCIS STOUGHTON, LL.D., Professor of Civil Law in Trinity College, Dublin, died in Aungier Street, Dublin, in 1766. [FDJ.4056]

SULLIVAN, JOHN, from Dublin, an indentured servant in Philadelphia, Pennsylvania, 1745. [EP.54]

SUMMERS, SAMUEL, a merchant, former apprentice to Isaac Summers, was admitted as a Freeman of Dublin in 1741, [DLA]; a merchant in Dublin, will, 1763, refers to his sousin Richard Summers in

Bristol, his brothers-in-law William Tuckett in Philipstown, County Carlow, Amos Strettell, and John Dawson a merchant in Dublin; his clerk Walter White, John Rook a calenderer in Dublin, his servant Edward Middleton; Christian Roeder clerk to Thomas Mulock a NP in Dublin, William Nobel, a gentleman in Dublin, and his clerk Richard Cudmore. [DRD]

SUMNER, W., a notary in Dublin, 1737. [PRONI.D354.432]

SWEENY, JOHN, a glue-boiler in Mill Street, Dublin, died 1766. [FDJ.4062]

SWEETMAN, CHRISTOPHER, a merchant, died in Thomas Street, Dublin, in 1766. [FDJ.4061]

SWEETMAN, MATTHEW, a merchant, was admitted as a Freeman of Dublin in 1615. [DLA]

SWEETMAN, THOMAS, a barber, formerly apprentice to William Leslie, was admitted as a Freeman of Dublin in 1751. [DLA]

SWEETMAN, Mrs, wife of John Sweetman a brewer and merchant in King Street near Stephen's Green, Dublin, died 1764. [FDJ.3929]

SWIFT, JAMES, a merchant in Dublin, will, 1749, wits John Richardson farmer of Arbour Hill, Dublin, George Smith at Arbour Hill, and Samuel Hattanville a merchant, John Lodge in Dublin. [DRD]

SYNOD, RICHARD, in Dublin, a lease, 1695. [PRONI.D552.B4.2.3]

SYNYRES, PETER, a gentleman in St George's Lane, parish of St Andrew, Dublin, in 1659. [C]

TACKER, THOMAS, in Stevens Street, Dublin, 1659. [C]

TADPOLE, JOHN, a blacksmith in Dublin, was denisized in Ireland in 1669. [IPR]; was admitted as a Freeman of Dublin in 1669. [DLA]

TALANT, PATRICK in Golden Lane, St Bride's parish, Dublin, 1659. [C]

TALBOT, ADAM, a merchant in Dublin, who was shipwrecked off Cornwall then robbed by the inhabitants in 1622. [CSPIre]

TALBOT, JOHN, born 1619, a merchant from Dublin, in Nantes, France, 1642, a witness before the High Court of the Admiralty of England in 1642. [TNA.HCA.58.239-240]

TALBOT, Lieutenant Colonel JOHN, a Roman Catholic officer in Dublin in 1693. [CSPDom.1693.16]; licensed to bear arms in 1705. [HMC.Ormonde.ii.477]

TALBOT, Colonel ....., of Belgard, a Roman Catholic officer in Dublin in 1693. [CSPDom.1693.16]

TALBOT, ..., son of Richard Talbot of Mallahide, was born in Molesworth Street, Dublin, in 1766. [FDJ.4096]

TAYLOR, ANNE, a widow in Dublin, probate 1687 PCC

TAYLOR, or MAPAS, CLARE, in Dublin, a certificate, 1691. [PRONI.D430.255]

TAYLOR, FRANCIS, in Dublin, a lease, 1601. [PRONI.D430.106]

TAYLOR, FRANCIS, son of Thomas Taylor in Dublin, a lease, 1627. [PRONI.D430.132]

TAYLOR, GEORGE, bond re a house in a lane of the High Street of Dublin, 1648. [PRONI.D430.153]

TAYLOR, JOSEPH, master of the Providence of Dublin bound for Barbados and Charleston, South Carolina, in 1768. [TNA.CO5.509]

TAYLOR, ROBERT, in Dublin, lease of a house on High Street, Dublin, in 1614. [PRONI.D430.118]; a bond re above, 1648. [PRONI.D430.153]

TAYLOR, THOMAS, and Mary Fitzsimmons, in Dublin, a marriage contract, 1604. [PRONI.D430.110]

TAYLOR, THOMAS, in Dublin, a receipt, 1626. [PRONI.D430.131]

TAYLOR, THOMAS, a joiner, was admitted as a Freeman of Dublin in 1654, [DLA]; a joiner and a brother of the Corporation of Carpenters in Dublin, 1656. [DCA.G2/1]

TAYLOR, THOMAS, in Dublin, probate 1683 PCC

TAYLOR, WILLIAM, a cooper, was admitted as a Freeman of Dublin in 1653, [DLA]; a cooper and a brother of the Corporation of Carpenters in Dublin, 1656. [DCA.G2/1]

TAYLOR, WILLIAM, a merchant, was admitted as a Freeman of Dublin in 1651, [DLA]; a merchant in Wine Tavern Street, Dublin, 1659. [C]

TAYLOR, Mrs, wife of Samuel Taylor gunner aboard HM Yacht Dorset, died in Anglesea Street, Dublin, in 1766. [FDJ.4112]

TEISSONIERE DE LA ROUVIERE, JEAN JACQUES, born in St Germain, Languedoc, France, a Huguenot soldier in the service of King William, died 1716 in Dublin. [HSP.XLI.67]

TEMPLE, HENRY, in Damask Street, St Andrews parish, Dublin, in 1659. [C]

TEMPLE, Sir JOHN, in Damask Street, St Andrews parish, Dublin, in 1659. [C]

TEMPLE, JOIIN, in Damask Street, St Andrews parish, Dublin, in 1659. [C]

TENNANT, JOHN, master of the Betty of Dublin trading with Charleston, South Carolina, in 1728. [New England Weekly Journal,83]

TERNAN, Mrs, wife of James Ternan a merchant, died in Bridge Street, Dublin, in 1766. [FDJ.4057]

TERRELL, WALTER, born 1600, a merchant in Dublin, a witness before the High Court of the Admiralty of England in 1641. [TNA.HCA.57.321]

THEOBALD, SAMPSON, Searcher, Gauger, and Packer at the port of Dublin in 1626. [CPRIre]

THOMAS, GEORGE, master of the Catherine of Dublin trading with Philadelphia, Pennsylvania, in 1804. [BM]

THOMAS, JONATHAN, a merchant in Dublin, was admitted as a burgess and guilds-brother of Glasgow in 1724. [GBR]

THOMAS, JOHN, born 1776 in Dublin, was naturalised in South Carolina in 1820. [NARA.M1183]

THOMAS, RICHARD, born 1681, an indentured servant from Dublin, bound for New England aboard the Virginia Merchant in 1698. [LRO]

THORNTON, JOHN, in Stevens Street, Dublin, 1659. [C]

THORNTON, WILLIAM, master of the Jane of Dublin trading with Virginia in 1699-1700. [ACV][TNA.CO5.1311][SPAWI.1700.234]

THORP, JOHN, born 1609, a sailor from Dublin, a witness before the High Court of the Admiralty of England, 1643. [TNA.HCA.58.443.510]

THWAITES, AUGUSTINE, an apothecary on Lower Ormond Quay, Dublin, married Miss Smith of Parliament Street, Dublin, in 1766. [FDJ.4120]

TIGHE, DANIEL, married Miss Blundell, sister of Reverend Dixie Blundell, in Frederick Street, Dublin, in 1764. [FDJ.3823]

TIGH, RICHARD, an alderman of Dublin in 1673. [SPDom.1673.527]

TIGHE, STERNE, a merchant, died on Usher's Quay, Dublin, in 1764. [FDJ.3815]

TIRRELL, JOHN, a carpenter, was admitted as a Freeman of Dublin in 1651, [DLA]; a carpenter and a brother of the Corporation of Carpenters in Dublin, 1656. [DCA.G2/1]

TISDALL, MARY, will, 1775, Dublin. [PRONI.T1075.37]

TISDALL, PHILIP, in Dublin, an agreement, 1736. [PRONI.D207.3.1]

TOOKE, BENJAMIN, a stationer and a member of the Guild of St Luke the Evangelist in 1669. [CSPIre]

TOOLE, FRANCIS, in Dublin, a Roman Catholic licensed to bear arms, 1705. [HMC.Ormonde.ii.477]

TOOLE, FRANCIS, master of the Betty and Sarah of Dublin trading between Glasgow and Guernsey in 1742. [NRS.E504.15.1]

TOOLE, GEORGE, a cooper, was admitted as a Freeman of Dublin in 1648, [DLA]; a cooper and a brother of the Corporation of Carpenters in Dublin, 1656. [DCA.G2/1]

TOOLE, THOMAS, a carpenter, was admitted as a Freeman of Dublin in 1634, [DLA]; Warden of the Corporation of Carpenters in Dublin, 1656. [DCA.G2/1]

TOOLE, ..., a grocer in Little Ship Street, Dublin, died in 1766. [FDJ.4042]

TOOLE, Mrs, wife of Laurence Toole a grocer, died in Thomas Street, Dublin, in 1766. [FDJ.4141]

TOTHILL, ROBERT, in Dublin, probate 1656 PCC

TOWERS, THOMAS, died in Henry Street, Dublin, in 1770. [FLJ.49]

TOWSON, WILLIAM, from Dublin, a mariner aboard HMS Jersey probate 1693 PCC

TRACY, DANIEL, in Bride Street, Dublin, died 1764. [FDJ.3832]

TRACY, Mrs, wife of James Tracy a china merchant, died in Fishamble Street, Dublin, in 1766. [FDJ.4115]

TRAMASIN, Mrs, wife of Michael Tramasin a merchant in Dublin, died in Stephen Street, Dublin, in 1766. [FDJ.4084]

TRAPAUD, JEAN, born in Chastillon, France, a Huguenot soldier in the service of King William, died in Dublin in 1733. [HSP.XLI.69]

TRAVERS, PETER, a merchant, was admitted as a Freeman of Dublin in 1640, [DLA]; a merchant in Bridge Street, Dublin, 1673. [SPDom.1673.527]

TRIMBLE, JOHN, master of the Two Friends of Dublin trading with Philadelphia, Pennsylvania, in 1736.[ICJ.IV.210]

TRIQUET, JOHN PETER, a silk dyer in Dublin, will, 1773, refers to his sister Lucy Roberdeau and Susanna Lecras in London, Isaac Roberdeau, John Combs and his wife Margaret also their daughter Mary in Meath Street, Dublin, John Carden, Mark Bloxham; wits. John Lennon a silk dyer in Dublin, Lewis Moore a gentleman in Dublin, George Cullen apprentice to said Lewis Moore, George Reynolds an apprentice to Lewis Moore. [DRD]

TROTTER, THOMAS, will, 1802, Dublin. [PRONI.T1075.37]

TRUYLE, Miss, in Stephen Street, Dublin, died in 1765. [FDJ.3935]

TUCKER, MARTIN, of Dublin, transported 1500 army recruits from Dublin to Portugal in 1704. [CTB.XIX.292/296]

TUCKER, THOMAS, a former Customs Collector in Dublin in 1659. [CSPIre]

TUCKER, Mrs, a widow, died in Mary Lane, Dublin, in 1766, sister of the Archbishop of Dublin. [FDJ.4078]

TUGWELL, CHRISTOPHER, master of the Hope of Dublin in 1667. [ActsPCCol]

TUITE, KATHERINE, in Dublin, pardoned of murder, 1625. [CPRIre]

TUIT, Lieutenant Colonel, a Roman Catholic officer in Dublin in 1693. [CSPDom.1693.16]

TURNER, ANNE, a widow in Dublin, a will, 1755, refers to sisters ... Palmer and .....Bernard, and to her nephew George Dunbar; wits her servant Thomas Groves, George More NP in Dublin and his clerk Edward Cullen. [DRD]

TURNER, ROBERT, a merchant from Dublin, emigrated to Pennsylvania in 1683. [EP.12]

TURNER, TIMOTHY, was admitted as a Freeman of Dublin in 1755, [DLA]; an ironmonger in Crown Alley, died 1764. [FDJ.3836]

TWELVES, Mrs, a midwife, born 1668, died in Fishamble Street, Dublin, in 1764. [FDJ.3790]

TYRELL, WALTER, born 1780, a surgeon and apothecary from Dublin, was naturalised in South Carolina in 1806. [NARA.M1183]

UNSTICE, Sir MORRIS, in Damask Street, St Andrews parish, Dublin, in 1659. [C]

UNTHANK, JOSHUA, a merchant, former apprentice to Henry Plunkett, was admitted as a Freeman of Dublin in 1719, [DLA]; a merchant in Dublin, co-owner of the Mary Ann of Liverpool registered at the Customs House of Liverpool in 1742.

UPTON, THOMAS, and his wife SARAH, in Dublin, a deed of mortgage, 1721. [PRONI.D264.1]

USHER, ARTHUR, in Dublin, a deed, 1627. [PRONI.D509.12][CPRIre]

USHER, ARTHUR, a merchant in Fishamble Street, St John's parish, Dublin, in 1659. [C]

USHER, Captain PATRICK, a Roman Catholic officer in Dublin in 1693. [CSPDom.1693.16]

USHER, ROBERT, Vice Provost of Trinity College, Dublin, in 1618. [CSPIre]

USHER, Sir WILLIAM, in Dublin, a deed, 1664. [PRONI.D1132.10.1.1]

USHER, Mrs, wife of John Usher a gentleman in Fleet Street, Dublin, died in 1764. [FDJ.3841]

VALANCE, JAMES, a book-seller in Grafton Street, Dublin, married Miss Wyer of Ballycurry, County Wicklow, in 1766. [FDJ.4109]

VANCE, JOHN, a merchant, was admitted as a Freeman of Dublin in 1768, [DLA]; a merchant in Abbey Street, Dublin, married ......Brown, daughter of James Brown, a merchant in Sackville Street, Dublin, in 1770. [FLJ.53]

VANDELEUR, FRANCES, in Dublin, married William Doyle a barrister at law, in 1766. [FDJ.4084]

VANDREMERE, HENRY, a painter and a publican in Anglesea Street, Dublin, died in 1764. [FDJ.3838]

VAN HOMRIGH, BARTHOMELEW, in Dublin, letters, 1695. [TCD.750.1428/2328]

VANTANDELO, THOMAS, a cabinet maker and upholder, died in Moor Street, Dublin, in 1765. [FDJ.3934]

VARANGLE, JEAN DE BARNIR, a Huguenot soldier in the service of King William, died in Dublin in 1728. [HSP.XLI.70]

VARNER, ABRAHAM, from London, then in Dublin, a will, 1747, mother Elizabeth Varner, wits. Robert Marshall, Michael Mockler a yeoman, Job Burnett an upholsterer, and Alexander Castell, all in Dublin. [DRD]

VELDON, PATRICK, master of the Mary Ann of Dublin trading between Ireland and Catelonia, Spain, in 1705. [TNA.SP42.119.193]

VERNER, THOMAS, in Dublin, a lease, 1750. [PRONI.D236.21]

VIDAUZE, PETER, a merchant in Fade Street, Dublin, died in 1764. [FDJ.3787]

THE PEOPLE OF DUBLIN, 1600-1799

VIDELL, JOHN, master of the John of Dublin trading with Virginia in 1724. [WI.22.23]

VIGNEAU, ISAAC, born 1691, a sugar baker, died in King Street, St Stephen's Green, Dublin, in 1766. [FDJ.4126]

VINCENT, WILLIAM, a senior fellow of Trinity College, Dublin, 1661. [CSPIre]

VIOLAS, NOAH, born 1676, a jeweller, former apprentice to John Sterne, was admitted as a Freeman of Dublin in 1717, [DLA]; a jeweller in Jervais Street, Dublin, married Miss Martha Champion, born 1686, of Stafford Street, Dublin in 1766. [FDJ.4068]

VIRASEL, JACQUES DE BELRIEU, a Huguenot who settled in Dublin before 1695, died there in 1719. [HSP.XLI.72]

VIRIDET, MOSES, the minister of the French Protestant church in Dublin in 1684. [CSPDom.1684.261]

VIZER, RALPH, in Dublin, later in Bristol, probate 1667 PCC

WADE, Lieutenant HENRY, in Skinner Row, parish of St Nicholas within the Walls, Dublin, in 1659. [C]

WADE, JAMES, a grocer, died in Skinner Row, Dublin, in 1764. [FDJ.3801]

WAIGHT, SILVESTER, a merchant in Skinner Row, parish of St Nicholas within the Walls, Dublin, in 1659. [C]

WAINHOUSE, JOSEPH, a weaver in the Comb, Dublin, a will, 1776, refers to his four children – Martha, Joshua, Elizabeth, and Richard, William Paine; wits. Michael Dowling a weaver in Dublin, John Chandler a weaver in Dublin, Patrick Smyth a gentleman in Dublin, and William Kelly a gentleman in Dublin. [DRD]

WAINWRIGHT, ANTHONY, a Fellow of Trinity College, Dublin, in 1618. [CSPIre]

WAINWRIGHT, ……., in Cornmarket, Dublin, died in 1766. [FDJ.4110]

WALKER, ABRAHAM, a cabinet maker, died in William Street, Dublin, in 1764. [FDJ.3808]

WALKER, FRANCES, daughter of the late Alderman William Walker, died in Claredon Street, Dublin, in 1764. [FDJ.3924]

WALKER, HENRY, in Dublin, a deed, 1665. [PRONI.D430.78]

WALKER, Mr, died on Lazer's Hill, Dublin, in 1764. [FDJ.3828]

WALLACE, NICHOLAS, master of the James of Dublin trading with Bilbao in Spain in 1705. [CalSPDom.SP44.390.323]

WALLACE, WILLIAM, a bookbinder of Meeting House Yard, Dublin, died 1766. [FDJ.4108]

WALLER, Mrs, died in Dirty Lane, Thomas Street, Dublin, in 1765. [FDJ.3932]

WALLIS, CHARLES and ELIZABETH, in Dublin, a lease, 1698. [PRONI.D580.4]

WALLIS, NICHOLAS, a joier, was admitted as a Freeman of Dublin in 1651, [DLA]; a joiner and a brother of the Corporation of Carpenters in Dublin, 1656. [DCA.G2/1]

WALSH, DENNIS, a robber, was executed at Stephen's Green, Dublin, in 1765. [FDJ.3932]

WALSH, GEOFFREY, Searcher and Gauger of the port of Dublin in 1626. [CPRIre]

WALSH, Lieutenant GEORGE, a Roman Catholic officer in Dublin in 1693. [CSPDom.1693.16]

WALSH, JOHN, of Ballyawley, Dublin, in 1611. [Carew ms]

WALSH, JOHN, a cooper and a brother of the Corporation of Carpenters in Dublin, 1656. [DCA.G2/1]; in Damask Street, St Andrews parish, Dublin, in 1659. [C]; a cooper and a member of the Fraternity of St Patrick's near Dublin in 1666. [CalSPIre]

WALSH, or ROURK, MARY, a widow in Dublin, a will, 1709. [DRD]

WALSH, OLIVER, a joiner, was admitted as a Freeman of Dublin in 1640, [DLA]; Master of the Corporation of Carpenters of Dublin in 1656. [DCA.G2.1]

WALSH, PATRICK, a mason, was admitted as a Freeman of Dublin in 1639, [DLA]; a mason and a brother of the Corporation of Carpenters in Dublin, 1656. [DCA.G2/1]

WALSH, ROBERT, a linen draper in Bride Street, Dublin, married Elizabeth Reilly of Rahattin, County Wicklow, in 1765. [FDJ.3932]

WALSH, THOMAS, of Abbey Street, Dublin, married Miss Connell of County Dublin, in 1766. [FDJ.4077]

WALSH, Colonel, a Roman Catholic officer in Dublin in 1693. [CSPDom.1693.16]

WALSH, Mrs, wife of Walter Walsh, master of the Globe Coffee House, died in Essex Street, Dublin, in 1764. [FDJ.3805]

WALTON, THOMAS, in Stevens Street, Dublin, 1659. [C]

WARBURTON, GEORGE, and JOHN WARBURTON, in Dublin, a lease, 1697. [PRONI.D3007.A13.62]

WARD, or PERCIVAL, Mrs ELIZABETH, a letter, 1760. [PRONI.D906.104]

WARD, BERNARD, and Miss Keegan, both of Bridge Street, Dublin, were married in 1766. [FDJ.4119]

WARDE, PETER, a cooper and a brother of the Corporation of Carpenters in Dublin, 1656. [DCA.G2/1]

WARD, RICHARD, a distiller and a brother of the Corporation of Carpenters in Dublin, 1656. [DCA.G2/1]; in St Bride's parish, Dublin, in 1659. [C]; a member of the Guild of Brewers in Dublin in 1669. [CSPIre]

WARD, Mrs, wife of Benjamin Ward a ribband weaver, died in Nicholas Street, Dublin, in 1763. [FDJ.3723]

WARD, ..., a painter in Nassau Street, Dublin, died 1764. [FDJ.38r36]

WARDEN, WILLIAM, possibly from Dublin, aboard HMS Lincoln, probate 1698 PCC

WARE, ARTHUR, in Dublin, a lease, 1617. [PRONI.D1390.27.1]

WARE, JAMES, in Dublin, a lease, 1617. [PRONI.D1390.27.1]

WARING, SAMUEL, in Dublin, a letter, 1699. [PRONI.D695.94]

WARREN, MARSDEN, a gentleman, married Lilly, daughter of Alexander Lilly, a jeweller on the Blind Quay, Dublin, in 1766. [FDJ.4081]

WARREN, THOMAS, and his son John, in Stevens Street, Dublin, 1659. [C]

WARREN, Lieutenant Colonel, in St Bride's parish, Dublin, in 1659. [C]

WARING, SAMUEL, in Dublin, a letter, 1699. [PRONI.D695.51]

WARING, SAMUEL, in William Street, Dublin, son of William Waring in Waringstown, a letter, 1699. [PRONI.D695.53]

WARREN, Captain ABLE, in Golden Lane, St Bride's parish, Dublin, 1659. [C]

WASSON, WILLIAM, from Dublin, died in Virginia, administration, 1733 PCC

WATERS, HENRY, Craner and Packer of the port of Dublin in 1625. [CPRIre]

WATSON, JOHN, born 1689, a comedian, died in Werburgh Street, Dublin, in 1766. [FDJ.4041]

WATSON, THOMAS, a merchant in Dublin, probate 1699 PCC

WATTS, JEREMY, a gentleman in Trinity Lane, College Green, Dublin, in 1659. [C]

WATT, JOHN, master of the Betty of Dublin trading with Charleston, South Carolina, in 1767. [TNA.CO5.511]

WATTS, THOMAS, in Dublin, a letter, 1674. [PROI.T3131.A43]

WATTS, WILLIAM, a merchant in Dublin, freighter of the St Francis of Antwerp which was shipwrecked near Portpatrick in Scotland, in 1666. [NRS.RH9.5.31]; a merchant, was admitted as a Freeman of Dublin in 1669. [DLA]

WATTSON, WILLIAM, in Dublin, a mortgage, 1709. [Inchiquin ms1273]

WEALE, WILLIAM, a plasterer, was admitted as a Freeman of Dublin in 1637, [DLA]; a plasterer and a brother of the Corporation of Carpenters in Dublin, 1656. [DCA.G2/1]

WEATHERS, ROBERT, from Dublin, later in London, a mariner aboard the Elisabeth, probate 1692 PCC

WEBB, JAMES, a merchant in Skinner Row, parish of St Nicholas within the Walls, Dublin, in 1659. [C]

WEBB, JAMES, in Dublin, a deed, 1732. [PRONI.D778.72A]

WEBBER, EDWARD, in Dublin, a letter, 1710. [PRONI.D2707.A1.1.1A]

WEEKES, NICHOLAS, in Dublin, a deed, 1755. [PRONI.D778.115]

WEILY, JOHN, a timber merchant on George's Quay, Dublin, died in 1766. [FDJ.4097]

WELDON, CHRISTOPHER, a merchant in Anderson's Court, Dublin, died in 1766. [FDJ.4053]

WELSH, ANTHONY, died in Rosemary Lane, Dublin, in 1764. [FDJ.3825]

WELSH, HUMPHREY, a prisoner in Dublin Castle in 1624. [CSPIre]

WELSH, JAMES, born 1602, a merchant in Dublin, a witness before the High Court of the Admiralty of England in 1625. [TNA.HCA13.45.23]

WENWELL, Sir GEORGE, in Damask Street, St Andrews parish, Dublin, in 1659. [C]

WESBY, WILLIAM, a gentleman in Damask Street, St Andrews parish, Dublin, in 1659. [C]

WEST, PATRICK, an apothecary, died in Fishamble Street, Dublin, in 1770. [FLJ.49]

WESTENRA, ..., son of Henry Westenra, was born in Sackville Street, Dublin, in 1766. [FDJ.4128]

WESTGARTH, WILLIAM, in Dublin, deeds, 1688/1692. [PRONI.D389.13; D509.31]

WESTON, NICHOLAS, a joiner and son of Oliver Weston a merchant, was admitted as a Freeman of Dublin in 1651, [DLA]; a joiner and a brother of the Corporation of Carpenters in Dublin, 1656. [DCA.G2/1]

WESTON, Alderman in Fishamble Street, St John's parish, Dublin, in 1659. [C]

WHALEY, JOHN, in Dublin, a lease, 1790. [PRONI.D308.4]

WHITE, ARCHIBALD, in Dublin, will, 1752, wife Jane Smith or White, daughters Margaret, Martha and Ann, cousins James White, Timothy White, and Archibald White son of Archibald White, Robert Dent, wits. Lawrence Lawrenson, Gerald Byrne, Francis McCollagh, yeomen, and Hugh Burnett, all in Dublin. [DRD]

WHITE, EDWARD, son of Thomas White a merchant, was admitted to the Merchant Guild of Dublin in 1601. [DGM]

WHITE, HUGH, a merchant, was admitted as a Freeman od Dublin in 1709, [DLA]; a merchant in Dublin, a charter party re a voyage to Trondheim, Norway, in 1720. [PRONI.D354.371]; trading with Cadiz, Spain, in 1728. [PRONI.D354.473]

WHITE, JAMES, master of the Hopewell of Dublin trading with Virginia in 1700. [TNA.CO5.1311]; master of the Joseph of Dublin trading between Dublin and Bilbao in Spain, 1705-1706. [TNA.SP44.393.20; SP63.366.63]

WHITE, JOHN, in Skinner Row, parish of St Nicholas within the Walls, Dublin, in 1659. [C]

WHITE, JOHN, born 1663, died in Bull Alley, Dublin, in 1764. [FDJ.3820]

WHITE, ROBERT, an attorney, died in Kevin Street, Dublin, in 1766. [FDJ.4132]

WHITE, THOMAS, in Dublin, a bond, 1647. [PRONI.D430.152]

WHITFIELD, HENRY, in Dublin, a lease of premises in the High Street of Dublin, 1680, [PRONI.D514.4]; probate 1689 PCC

WHITFIELD, HESTER, a widow in Dublin, probate 1699 PCC

WHITGROVE, THOMAS, in Francis Street, St Patrick's parish, Dublin, in 1659. [C]

WHITTINGHAM, Dr CHARLES, in George's Lane, Dublin, a letter, 29 March 1728. [TCD.750.2179]

WIGHT, WILIAM, a Presbyterian minister in Mary's Abbey, Capel Street, Dublin, 1753. [F.7.533]

WILCOX, NICHOLAS, in Skinner Row, parish of St Nicholas within the Walls, Dublin, in 1659. [C]

WILKINSON, OLIVER, a brazier, married Miss Fisher of Cutpurse Row, Dublin, in 1764. [FDJ.3846]; a brazier, was admitted as a Freeman of Dublin in 1772. [DLA]

WILKINSON, WILLIAM, master of the Boyne of Dublin trading with Virginia in 1752, also in 1770. [TNA.CO5.1320.R3/14;43] [VaGaz.80][PaGaz.2188]

WILKS, THOMAS, master of the Marcella of Dublin trading with Bilbao in Spain in December 1705. [TNA

WILLCOCKS, ISACHER, a Quaker merchant in Dublin, son of Joshua Willcocks, was admitted as a Freeman of Dublin in 1720, [DLA]; was admitted as a burgess and guilds-brother of Glasgow in 1724. [GBR]

WILLCOCKS, THOMAS, a Quaker merchant, was admitted as a Freeman of Dublin in 1698. [DLA]

WILLES, JOHN, a distiller in Dublin, probate 1699, PCC

WILLES, Miss, daughter of Joshua Willes, died on Usher's Quay, Dublin, in 1764. [FDJ.3789]

WILLIAMS, JOHN, a turner, former apprentice of Rowland Williams a turner, was admitted as a Freeman of Dublin in 1692. [DLA]

WILLIAMS, JOSHUA, a Quaker weaver in Cole's Alley, Dublin, was admitted as a Freeman of Dublin in 1742. [DLA]

WILLIAMS, LEWIS, a carpenter and a brother of the Corporation of Carpenters in Dublin, 1656. [DCA.G2/1]

WILLIAMS, THOMAS, a cooper and a brother of the Corporation of Carpenters in Dublin, 1656. [DCA.G2/1]

WILLIAMS, THOMAS, a currier in Nicholas Street, Dublin, died in 1766. [FDJ.4097]

WILLIAMSON, JAMES, a grocer in Pill Lane, Dublin, married Peggy Grierson, in Dublin in 1770, daughter of John Grierson of Doolistown, County Meath. [FLJ.49]

WILLIAMSON, JOHN, of the City of London, died in Dublin, probate 1686 PCC

WILLIAMSON, JOHN, in Dublin, a lease, 1726. [PRONI.D552.1.1.133]

WILLIAMSON, WILLIAM, a gilder, died in Hoey's Court, Dublin, in 1764. [FDJ.3803]

WILLOUGHBY, SYMON, a tallow chandler, was admitted as a Freeman of Dublin in 1693. [DLA]

WILLOUGHBY, WYNDHAM, a baker, was admitted as a Freeman of Dublin in 1758, [DLA]; a druggist in Capel Street, Dublin, died in 1766. [FDJ.4112]

WILSON, GEORGE, an apothecary in Bride Street, Dublin, formerly an apprentice of George Wilson a merchant burgess, was admitted a Freeman of Dublin in 1755. [DLA]

WILSON, JAMES, born 1782, a physician from Dublin, naturalised in South Carolina in 1806. [NARA.M1183]

WILSON, ROBERT, a skinner, formerly an apprentice of John Wilson, was admitted as a Freeman of Dublin in 1765. [DLA]

WILSON, THOMAS, a tallow chandler, died in George's Lane, Dublin, in 1764. [FDJ.3822]

WINDER, EDWARD, in Dublin Customs House, a letter, 1800. [PRONI.D572.8.40]

WINNET, CLEMENT, an attorney in Dublin, died in 1766. [FDJ.4040]

WINTERINGHAM, CHRISTOPHER, a gentleman in Dublin, probate 1688 PCC

WILSON, R., master of the Boyne of Dublin trading with Pennsylvania in 1770. [PaGaz.2188]

WOGAN, THOMAS, master of the Mary of Dublin, trading between Youghal and Bilbao, Spain, in 1705. [TNA.SP44.390.350]

WOLFE, THOMAS, formerly a trader on Bridge Street, Dublin, died on Merchants Quay, Dublin, in 1763. [FDJ.3726]

WOODHOUSE, or WIDDOWER, JOHN, a gentleman in Dublin, died in London, probate 1654 PCC

WOODS, Captain DANIEL, a Roman Catholic officer in Dublin in 1693. [CSPDom.1693.16]

WOODS, HENRY, a barber surgeon, formerly an apprentice of Joseph Woods, was admitted as a Freeman of Dublin in 1712. [DLA]

WOODS, ROBBIE, a brewer, spouse of Margaret Foros, was admitted as a Freeman of Dublin in 1663. [DLA]

WOODS, WILLIAM, died in Arran Street, Dublin, in 1766. [FDJ.4068]

WOODWARD, THOMAS, a plasterer and a brother of the Corporation of Carpenters in Dublin, 1656. [DCA.G2/1]

WOODWARD, ..., a tailor in Winetavern Street, Dublin, died in 1766. [FDJ.4041]

WORSOP, Sir THOMAS, in Dublin, died in Chester, probate 1689 PCC

WORTH, WILLIAM, in Dublin, an indenture, 1699. [AC]

WRIGHT, HENRY, in Dublin, probate 1664. [PRONI.T3765.21]

WRIGHT, JOHN, a joiner and a brother of the Corporation of Carpenters in Dublin, 1656. [DCA.G2/1]; a joiner, was admitted as a Freeman of Dublin in 1654. [DLA]

WRIGHT, TIMOTHY, from Dublin, an indentured servant in Philadelphia, Pennsylvania, 1745. [EP.55]

WRIGHT, Lieutenant, in Sheep Street, St Bride's parish, Dublin, 1659. [C]

WYBRANTZ, DANIEL, sr., an Alderman of Dublin, a Dutch subject, who was naturalised in Ireland, along with his wife Elizabeth and sons Daniel, Peter, and Henry, however Daniel sr died in Holland before 1673. [SPDom.1673.500]

WYBRANTZ, PETER, a merchant in Dublin in 1631; an Alderman of Dublin in 1660; a merchant who petitioned King Charles II about trade with the Canary Islands in 1666. [CSPIre][GAR.ONA.42.109.172]

WYNNE, Colonel JAMES, in Dublin, a letter, 1694. [PRONI.D429.90]

WYNELL, THOMAS, from Goldhanger in Essex, died in Dublin, probate 1698 PCC

YARNER, ABRAHAM, in Dublin, Muster Master General of H.M. Forces in Ireland, probate 1700 PCC

YARNER, JANE, a spinster in Church Street, Dublin, will, 1753, wits. Ann Green a spinster, Adam Sharply an innkeeper, and Arthur Parker a gentleman, all of Dublin. [DRD]

YEATES, JOHN, a silk weaver, died in Francis Street, Dublin, in 1764. [FDJ.3800]

YOUNG, MATTHEW, of Francis Street, Dublin, married ..... Traynor, in 1770. [FLJ.51]

www.ingramcontent.com/pod-product-compliance
Lightning Source LLC
Chambersburg PA
CBHW070921270326
41927CB00011B/2670